PRACTICAL
PASTORAL MANUAL

This manual includes summarized teachings and guidelines from the Harvest Army International Seminary for new pastors and leaders of churches. This is not an exhaustive minister's manual, but focuses on areas needed for new pastors and ministry leaders to lead a church and conduct pastoral ministry. This is the second version. Regular updates and subsequent versions may be released.

Practical Pastoral Manual

Compiled by Harvest Army International Seminary, Stone Mountain, GA.

Version.2 (June 3, 2021).

Copyright © 2021 by Harvest Army International Seminary

ISBN 978-1-7334859-9-9

TABLE OF CONTENTS

- CHURCH GROWTH STRATEGIES 5
- DEVELOPING AN EFFECTIVE ORDER OF SERVICE 33
- CREATING A PURPOSEFUL YEARLY PLAN 43
- INCREASING THE IMPACT OF YOUR MINISTRY 53
- FOSTERING AN EVANGELISTIC CHURCH 69
- BASIC DISCIPLESHIP TRAINING 75
- MINISTERING DELIVERANCE EFFECTIVELY 87
- TIPS ON PASTORAL COUNSELING 99
- MINISTERING THE BAPTISM OF THE SPIRIT 117
- BECOMING A PROPHETIC CHURCH 123
- OFFICIATING A WEDDING 135
- CONDUCTING THE LORD'S SUPPER 141
- WASHING OF THE SAINTS' FEET 145
- PERFORMING BAPTISMS 149
- PERFORMING FUNERALS 155
- BABY DEDICATION 159
- CONDUCTING A GENERAL MEMBER'S MEETING 163

CONDUCTING A BOARD MEETING 167

TIPS FOR RESOLVING CONFLICTS 171

HANDLING CHURCH FINANCES 179

LAYING ON OF HANDS 183

MISCELLANEOUS SUGGESTIONS AND ADMONITIONS 191

HOW TO USE THIS BOOK

It is best to use this book as a reference for your pastoral ministry needs. It handles the 'how to' questions of pastoring. The first ten chapters are about growing your church and ministering to others. The next six chapters are about conducting certain ceremonies or sacraments. The next four chapters deal with the administrative aspects of church leadership. The final two chapters include laying on of hands and suggestions for the pastor. Go to the chapter you need when you are dealing with any of these areas. E-mail info@harvestarmy.org for any further questions.

1
CHURCH GROWTH STRATEGIES

Every pastor should know the basic strategies that are necessary to grow a church. It takes more than just dedication for a church to grow. Under the leading and power of the Holy Spirit, the pastor must apply certain skills for a church to grow. In this chapter, we review the skills that are necessary for the growth of a church.

FOUNDATIONAL PRINCIPLES ON CHURCH GROWTH

- Human power and wisdom cannot produce quality church growth. The pastor must rely on the power of the Holy Spirit.
    - The power of the Holy Spirit was the chief ingredient in the growth of the first church (Acts 1 - 4).
    - The demonstration of the power of God draws the attention of unbelievers (Acts 2 – 4, 8).
    - The Holy Spirit directs the church in ministry (Acts 13-14).

- We must preach the full truth of the Word of God. Compromising God's Word to attract members will not produce Biblical church growth. We can have confidence that the Bible is reliable. We know the Bible is true because:
    o It matches the original manuscripts or texts.
    o It has the power to change lives.
    o God honors it.
    o Manuscripts of Bible texts are still available in the original languages (Hebrew and Greek) and verify the accuracy of today's copies.
    o As more manuscripts are found, they confirm the text.
- The pastor must recognize the move of God among the people. For example, recognize when God is moving among a group of people, community, city, or nation in a specific way (a call for repentance, healing, and miracles, outpouring of the Spirit, a prophetic word, etc.).
- One must recognize the waves of the Holy Spirit.
    o The Holy Spirit will move in the church in a special way. Recognizing the wave, the move of the Spirit, and cooperating with the Spirit in that move will produce growth.
    o The wave refers to a massive spiritual movement among the people. It could be a realization of God meeting a spiritual need

among the people or God stirring the hearts of the people. The wave may also be God drawing people to a certain place or location for a move of His Spirit.

- o Man cannot create a wave. Man can only catch the growth wave already given by God and ride it.

- o Being prayerful, sensitive to the Holy Spirit, and stepping out boldly to the Spirit's leading will help you to catch the wave.

- o To recognize and catch the wave takes insight, patience, faith, and skill. Insight to see what God is doing; patience to allow God to move; faith to see it through; skill to lead others in the move through to the Spirit.

- o By the leading of the Spirit, we must be skilled-experts in catching the wave. Jesus is the master builder (1 Cor.3:6). We build on His foundation. As God moves, we build.

- o In times of crisis, people hunger for God. You may see a wave of the Spirit as people cry out to God, and God meets their needs. Through the Spirit, skillfully build the church on this wave.

MYTHS ABOUT INCREASING THE FLOCK

Many pastors make incorrect conclusions about church growth. These false conclusions are often built based on criticisms of larger churches. Every pastor must evaluate their personal biases that hinder the ability to grow a church. Check the myths below, eradicate them from your mind, and apply the correct principles for growth.

Myth #1: Attendance is the only concern of large churches.

Many large churches do not overemphasize attendance. They instead have developed and mastered the skill to **settle** those in **attendance**:

- Being unique about what the church offers based on God's vision and revelation for that church. Also, every church has been given a unique set of gifts and available resources.
- Mainly positive faith-building preaching.
- Uplifting preaching balanced with correction and rebuke only when necessary.
- Keeping the members abreast and excited about the direction where the church is going.
- Ensuring that members can bring visitors and not feel embarrassed.

- Designing plans to build and expand.
- Training and sending workers.
- Offering something they cannot get anywhere else based on the church's gifts, abilities, resources and vision. Examples include an unusual vision for growth, teachings on topics rarely covered, unique gifts in the church, a special youth ministry, etc.

Busting this Myth

Growth must be in different dimensions: Warm, Deep, Strong, Broad, Large.

- Warm through Fellowship
- Deep through Discipleship
- Strong through Worship
- Broad through Ministry
- Large through Evangelism

Myth #2: That all large churches grow at the expense of small churches.

Busting this Myth

Many large churches grew by:

- Much soul winning. Most converts got saved in that church.
- A massive geographic relocation: a large movement of people to a new area or location.
- Quality ministry
- Focusing on the vision.

Myth #3: Quantity is more important than quality.

Busting this Myth

Many large churches emphasize quality by:

- The kind of disciples
- Transformation
- Maturation
- Evangelizing

Myth #4: Large churches must compromise the message and mission to grow.

Busting this Myth

Matthew 9:37 shows that the harvest is plentiful. It is laborers that are lacking. The passage from Matthew 9:35-38 shows that as Jesus demonstrated the power of God and taught that the people followed him.

Rather, growth naturally occurs when the church speaks and manifests the truth in the power of God. The dying churches in the Western world are those that are compromising the Word of God. The growing churches, such as some from the Pentecostal/Charismatic movement, hold to the truth of God's Word.

Myth #5: If there is dedication, the church will grow.

Busting this Myth

Growth is by:

- Skill
- Being Smart
- Willing to learn from successful models (1 Cor.3:10).
- Churches grow by the power of God and through the skill and effort of the people.

Myth #6: There is one secret key to church growth.

No, it is a complex matter. One factor seldom causes it. We must always be willing to apply another method.

Myth #7: All God expects of us is faithfulness.

Ministers must be both faithful and **fruitful**. Here success involves bearing as much fruit as possible with the gifts, opportunities and potentials they have.

- God calls us to bear fruit John 15:16.
- Fruitlessness brings God's judgment
- Being fruitful glorifies God
- Fruitfulness is evidence of the calling

Myth #8: That you cannot learn from large churches:

You can learn the following from large churches:

- Principles
- Process
- Methods

PURPOSE OF THE CHURCH

For the church to grow, the pastor must know the general purpose of the church. And, the pastor should know and effectively communicate the unique purpose of the local church he leads.

5 Purposes of the Church

1. Love the Lord with all your heart. Ps 34:3, Matt. 4:10.
2. Love your **neighbors** as yourself Eph. 4: 12
3. Go and make disciples Acts 1:8, Matt. 28:19-20. Job 20:21.
4. Baptism - baptizing them Eph. 2:19
5. Teaching them to obey Col. 1:28, John 17, Eph. 4: 1-16.

4 Main Things to Know

1. The church must have a clear-cut identity.
2. Reason for being.
3. Know what should be omitted.
4. Precise purpose.

- A solid foundation needs a <u>clear statement of purpose:</u>
  - It builds morals (1 Cor.1:10).
  - It reduces frustration.
  - It allows concentration.
  - It attracts cooperation.
  - It assists with evaluation.

Making a Purpose Statement

- It must be Biblical.
- It must be **specific** (simple and clear).
- It must be **transferable**.
- It must be **measurable.**

<u>Example</u>: Harvest Army International Seminary's Mission Statement:

The mission of HAIS is to train and equip men and women of God for impactful ministry and dedicated service in today's society. 'Ministers' in this context include all believers who have answered the call of God. Our vision is to:

1. Provide a wholesome foundation in Biblical doctrine that will prepare ministers to effectively proclaim and defend the Christian faith.

2. Equip and train ministers to plant and lead ministries that are centered upon God's mandate for the current time, thereby being catalysts for world revival.

3. Prepare and produce Christian leaders that demonstrate integrity and spiritual authority in their personal lives and ministry, in the midst of growing ethical issues that challenge the church.

4. To prepare Christian leaders to be effective in representing Christ in all aspects of society.

HOW TO ATTRACT THE CROWD

Having a crowd does not necessarily mean that the church is growing. Churches grow as it gains new members who remain. However, attracting the crowd is necessary to reach those whom God will add to your church. Therefore, pastors should ensure under God that they are doing the things that will draw the crowd.

Jesus attracted the crowd by:

1. Loving them (Matt: 9:30, Luke 7:34). Jesus' love was centered towards sinners.
2. Meeting their Needs (Matt 15:30)
3. Teaching them
4. Strong Leadership
5. Effective Worship
6. Designing Effective Services

Loving Them

Needs for love:

- Acceptance
- Forgiveness
- Self-expression
- Purpose for living
- Freedom from bondages such as guilt, worry, resentment, discouragement, loneliness, etc.

Ways for a pastor to be loving

- Memorize the names of people.

- Greet the people personally before and after service.
- Touch the people: a word, handshake, pat, hug.
- Write personally to the people (Associate Ministers should do it also).

How to Love Unbelievers Like Jesus Did:

- Creating an atmosphere of acceptance.
  - Church willing to go where they are.
  - Members park off-campus so visitors can park
  - Members stand so visitors can sit
  - Offer their coat to those who have not
  - Correct the people in love
  - Forgive them
  - Be impartial
  - Keep troublemakers in church
  - Maintain bridges after separation
  - Motivate them
- Visitors feel members are **friendly**.
  - Find out how they will get home?
  - Arrange transportation.
  - Offer help where needed while remaining non-intrusive.
- Preferred seating or assistance
- Accepting without approving:

- Samaritan woman, Zacchaeus, adulterous woman.
- Gathering of the crowd beyond membership.
- Gathering of the Congregation (1 Cor 5:9-12).

Meeting their Needs (the way Jesus did)

- Discover the key to their heart by asking questions without being intrusive
- Offer them what they cannot get anywhere else: e.g.
  - Coffee or Tea
  - A small gift
  - Assistance with parking
  - Short tour of the ministry
  - A candy, mint etc.
  - Wake up call for children
  - Free baby dedication
  - Free or reduced-price for baby care among members
  - Free weddings
  - Free or thrift items
- Establish Ministries around unique needs:
  - Free educational classes and Bible classes
  - Sidewalk Sunday School
  - To couples dealing with miscarriage.
  - Peacemaker
  - Hope for the separated and other marriage problems.

- - Lifeline; help
  - Troubled teenagers
- Celebrate recovery (from drugs, alcohol etc.)
- Build Trust in the local **community**

Teaching in Practical Interesting Ways

- Jesus taught the crowd too. Mark 10:1).
- The secret to Jesus' powerful teaching and preaching was that he operated in the power of the Holy Spirit. With that in mind, Teaching and Preaching must:
- Be **Problem Solving**: (What is the most pressing problem? Where are issues pressing people the most?
  - Provide timely answers. Answer immediately.
  - Answer in a relevant manner
- Be Amazing: Mark 1:27
- Be Enthusiastic: Mark.11:17-18
- Be Enjoyable: Mark.12:37
- Be Astonishing: Mark.11:18
- Delivered in an effective style (style is as important as content)

Strong Leadership

- Vision: for where they want to church to go.

- Conviction: an inner assurance or confidence in what you believe.
- Unquenchable Passion
- Respect-based relationships with members, visitors and colleagues
- Effective Communication Skills
- Strategic Mind
- Purposeful Courage
- Effective Delegation: (Preaching, Counseling, Fundraising, Evangelism)

Effective Worship

Pastors with a church growth mindset will foster worship services that are sensitive to unbelievers and visitors seeking something from God. A 'seeker sensitive' church looks to reach and impact the unbeliever in attendance, avoiding behaviors that may unnecessarily turn the unbeliever away from the church. Remember that one of the main goals of the church is to win unbelievers to Christ. We reject the idea and trend among some "seeker-sensitive churches" that compromise the truth and allow worldliness. A church can be "seeker-sensitive" while maintaining truth and holiness.

When designing a 'seeker-sensitive' worship service, consider these:

- Only believers can worship.

- You don't need a building to worship God.
- There is no correct style of worship.
- Unbelievers cannot worship, but they can sense the impact.
- Worship is a powerful witness.
- God expects us to be sensitive to the unbeliever's fears, struggles and needs and be willing to modify the service if more unbelievers are present. The message, however, does not need to be compromised. Answer questions unbelievers wrestle with:
    o Who am I?
    o Where did I come?
    o Where am I going?
    o Does life make sense?
    o Why is there suffering and evil in the world?
    o What is my purpose in life?
    o How can I get along with people?
    o What is God like?
    o How do I forgive others?
    o How do I strengthen my marriage?
- The needs of believers and unbelievers often overlap.
- There is no standard way to design a 'Seeker Service'.
- Tailoring your services according to their purpose is best.

- A service geared towards seekers is meant to supplement personal evangelism.
- It takes unselfish, mature believers to offer a seeker sensitive service.
- Build anticipation among leaders, workers and members through prayer and fasting for upcoming services.
- Worship services are the times for the pastor, leader, and committed members to worship and minister out of the communion we have had with God.
- Prayer during 'seeker-sensitive services' are geared toward ministering to the needs of unbelievers, visitors, and members seeking God for a need. This is not the best time to build the prayer life of the church, but rather where the pastor and key workers of the church minister out of a thriving prayer life.

Designing Effective Services

Most churches rarely attract unbelievers. A crowd is not the church, but it is necessary for a large church. Members must invite people to visit. Members are uncomfortable to bring them to church because:

- The message is unpredictable.
- Services are not designed for unbelievers.
- Embarrassed of the quality of service.

Ineffective Ways used to Attract the Crowd:

- Using guilt to motivate members to invite others to the church.
- Large sign
- Just calling homes.
- Telemarketing
- Advertising

Effective Ways to Attract the Crowd – (The Practical Way)

- Target: Plan the service with your target in mind. Never let go of why you have service.
- Ease: Make it as easy as possible for the seeker visitor to attend.
    - Offer multiple service times.
    - Surplus Parking
    - Children Sunday school or similarities
    - Put a map of your church on the pamphlet
- <u>Pace</u>: Improve the pace of the **service**.
    - Minimize transitional time in the service.
    - Ensure the timing of each item on the program is appropriate.
- Flow: Improve the flow impact
    - Inspire (upbeat) movement
    - Praise (joyful songs)
    - Adoration (meditation)

- Commitment to act on the sermon.
- Tie it all together

- Comfort: Make visitors feel comfortable
  - Reserve the best parking spot (for first-time visitors)
  - Station greeters outside, inside (greeters, ushers).
  - Parking attendance
  - Set up an information table outside.
  - Posting of directional signs
  - Have music playing
  - Allow visitors to remain anonymous
  - Have registration cards available
  - Offer public welcome that relaxes the people.

- Environment: Brighten up the environment
  - Proper landscaping
  - Lighting
  - Sound
  - Seating
  - Space
  - Appropriate temperature
  - Plants (make the people feel alive).
  - Nursery (clean safe nurseries).
  - Clean restrooms (fresh smell).
  - Fix defects: painting, carpeting, sound, restrooms, seating

- Atmosphere: Creating an attractive atmosphere
    - Good Mood
    - Good spirit
    - Good Tone
    - Celebratory Music
- Expectation: How do we create expectation?
    - Create expectation through praying, intercession. Cause members to feel - enthusiastic about inviting guests.
    - Members praying about service upcoming
    - Move the faith of the people
    - Celebration
    - Affirmation
    - Information
    - Restoration
    - Liberation
- Simplify: Print a simple order of service
- Shortened Announcement: (train members to read bulletin)
- Evaluation: Continue to evaluate and seek to improve.
    - Feedback cards/suggestion box
    - Welcome cards
    - Worship evaluation
    - Remember who we are serving

EFFECTIVE LEADERSHIP

Strong leadership is necessary for growth. The following are some basics to develop effective leadership.

- The responsibility of the pastor must be focused and limited. The pastor should:
    - Be able to articulate the vision.
    - Own the vision.
    - Identify and develop teams.
    - Build cross-organizational relationships
    - Identify ministry opportunities.
    - Create opportunities.
    - Accumulate resources.
    - Create strategic plans.
    - Solve major problems.
    - Resolve major conflicts.
    - Communicating important information.
    - Evaluate the quality of the ministry.
- The pastor must be the primary **change driver**.
    - Model the change (personal appearance, preaching style, etc.)
    - Depend on other ministry leaders
    - Main leaders must carry the same change (culture). This:
        - Clarifies the change

- - Reinforces the change
  - Reduces conflict
  - Support the effect of the change.
  - Effective leaders push the church on the edge of the comfort zone.

- The pastor must exclude himself from most decisions and instead delegate.

  - It will bring smooth flow more rapidly
  - Delegation will be effective when the pastor is secure. The leader is aware of maximizing the time by using competent leaders and an effective system to monitor the church's impact and effectiveness.

EQUIPPING THE FAMILY

Every effective pastor realizes the impact of equipping families. Families are an essential building block of a growing church. Church leaders must know how to effectively minister to families and nurture them into becoming strong families. Strong families continually bring growth to a local church. Conversely, when families fall apart, it often leads to someone in the family leaving the church. Therefore, it is crucial that the church ministers to the various family needs that exist.

- General Statistics on Families

- 1/5 of families are productive.
  - 1/3 of families survive.
  - 1/2 of families are struggling with areas of failure, communication, finance, and sexuality.
- Needs of the Families:
  - Trusted counselors
  - Family mentors
  - True partnership
  - Handling frustrations
  - Handling disagreements.
  - Raising children
  - Post children life
  - Better child development skills
  - Moral values
  - Self-esteem
  - Emotional support.
  - Spiritual clarity
  - Relational empathy
- Teenagers want:
  - Happiness
  - Tightly knit environment
  - To be loved
  - To be relevant
  - Relevant changes
  - Source of belonging
  - Unconditional love
  - Effective communication with parents

- Genuine respect
- Acceptance of their peers
- Closeness in family
- Parental respect for each other
- Less financial stress
- Physical safety

- Role of the Church
  - Addressing needs of the entire family
  - Equipping the families for self-development
  - Provide clear standards
  - To assist in goals and plans
  - Mentors and coaches
  - Pastor as advocate
  - Seeking God's blessing
  - Provide standards for evaluation of healthy families.
  - Unspeakable truth
  - Provide accountability
  - Involve women in ministry to the family
  - Value family ministry
  - Create ministry opportunities.

Protestant churches are doing a good job:

- Teaching Biblical principles
- Christian counseling
- Norms in the families
- Prayer for the needs

LATEST CHURCH GROWTH TRENDS

Growing churches today are those that are applying one or more of the following. Every pastor must endeavor to follow the vision that God has given for their church. The God-given vision for your church is what makes it unique and brings growth. All of the following trends are practices that churches can incorporate to accomplish their vision.

- Accommodating a Multicultural Congregation
    - Meeting needs of a diverse cultural population
    - Incorporating different cultures where possible (in workers, activities, leadership)
- Making Remarkable Sacrifices
    - To train and deploy new leaders
    - To train and deploy missionaries
    - To plant daughter churches
- Fostering Healthy Family Relationships
- Offering Multiple Services
    - Sunday School
    - Sunday Morning Worship Service
    - Sunday Night Service

- Weeknight Prayer Meetings
- Mid-Week Service (possibly focused on teaching)
- New Convert Classes/Other Type of Spiritual Growth Classes
- Youth Service
- Periodic Revivals/Revival (At least once every 1-3 months)

- Having a vibrant online ministry
  - Social Media: Facebook, Twitter, etc.
  - Online videos – YouTube
  - Live Streaming
  - Podcasts

- Offering effective children and youth ministries
- Offering services specifically geared to non-members.
  - Uplifting concerts
  - Lectures and seminars on practical matters (marriage, family, financial health, etc.)
  - Special outreach services (revivals, revivals, block services, street meetings, etc.)

- Cultivating vibrant lay/member involvement in services
  - Offer multiple activities in services where members can participate

- Fostering Small Groups (Cell Groups)

2
DEVELOPING AN EFFECTIVE ORDER OF SERVICE

PRE-SERVICE CONSIDERATIONS

The pastor should arrive early to the church or designate another ministry leader to arrive an hour before the service to ensure the presentation of the church property is at its highest standard. A team from the church should clean and improve the sanctuary from the previous day. Both the exterior and the interior of the church property should be at the highest standard possible to show forth the glory of God.

It is beneficial for the pastor to have a team arrive early at the church at least 30 minutes in advance to pray for the Lord to move in the service. It could even be the pastoral team that meets together to pray before the start of the service.

ORDER OF SERVICE

The order of service may vary from church to church based on spiritual needs, culture, and the type of service. However, the following are healthy components that should be part of an effective service. The flow of the service should maximize the focus on worship and the Word of God. It's best to arrange the service to alternate between singing, reports, testimonies, and other items to keep an upbeat flow. Build an atmosphere of expectancy for the Holy Spirit to flow freely. The preaching of the Word should be the main highlight of the service. The service should allow for the involvement of multiple people so that different gifts are present in the service.

Include the following segments in a typical Sunday Morning Service and other similar services.

- Prayer/Consecration
    - For Sunday morning services geared towards the public, prayer and consecration should be **brief (5 - 10 minutes)** unless otherwise being specifically directed by the Spirit.
    - Encourage workers to consecrate themselves in prayer prior to the Sunday morning service, especially leaders in the church.
- Scripture reading
    - Short Passage
    - Clear and loud reading
- Singing and Music

- Designate a Praise and Worship Team and a Praise and Worship Leader.
- If possible, avoid having lead singers who are not gifted in singing and music.
- Let the Praise and Worship Team use songs that the congregation can take part in. Otherwise, have the words of the song on a screen so that the congregation can join in singing.
- Develop a choir where possible and include them in the order of service
- Solo Performances - allow gifted singers in the church to perform where possible.
- Singing/Musical Teams - allow gifted groups to flourish in the church and include them in the program.

- Welcome
  - The moderator/person leading the service should take the time to welcome any visitors and guests.
  - Generally, build an atmosphere where the members are welcoming of each other and any visitors and guests.

- Reports/Testimonies
  - Allow members eager to testify to share what God is doing in their life. Their testimony of miracles, salvation, financial blessings and

victory over temptation will build the faith of others, building expectancy in the service.
- Evangelistic Reports
    - Positive reports from weekly outreach
    - Worldwide Vision Day Reports – a day when believers worldwide unite in evangelizing in their community on the same day and time (worldwidevisionday.org).
- Prophetic Reports - reports of prophecies spoken and their fulfillments (Example: *Revelation Fireside*)
- Ministry Reports
    - Reports from powerful and impactful church events
    - New Church Plants
- Exhortations
    - Joshua Hour – give a chance to new and upcoming speakers to share a short word of exhortation.
    - Greetings/Short Sharing - asking ministers and other leaders to share a brief word to the church.

- Offering and Tithes
    - Share a Short Word on the blessings and responsibility of giving before calling for the congregation to give.
    - Motivate the people to give their best by faith.
    - Tithing - explain to the audience that tithe is 10% of their earnings. Tithe is a Biblical principle that existed before the law - Abraham, Jacob, and Isaac gave tithes by faith. Jesus also reinforced not to forget to tithe.
    - Have a system in place that encourages all to give their offering and tithes
        - Tithes and offering envelopes available to all members and visitors
        - A simple system of giving the offering - either ushers directing all seated to go up to the offering basket or the passing of the offering basket to each person.
        - Avoid treating the offering as something to get out of the way quickly. Rather, treat it as a vital spiritual aspect of the church service. Connect giving offerings and tithes to the spiritual well-being and growth of the people.
        - Highlight testimonies of God's blessings upon faithful givers, and reports of what the giving of people have accomplished in the ministry.

- Sermon

    - Opening Word - an initial message from a minister or other spiritual leader

    - Central Word - the main sermon

    - Closing Word/Altar Call - an admonition to the church before closing; a final short word to call unbelievers to the altar for salvation.

    - A basic sermon outline is available at the end of this chapter.

- Other Worship and Ministry Items

    - Poems and Recitals

    - Skits and Theatrical Performances

- Benediction

    - A pronouncement of blessing upon the church from a pastoral leader.

    - Some scriptural benedictions are at the end of this chapter.

BASIC SERMON OUTLINE

The sermon is the climax of the service. Spending time with God is a non-negotiable part of receiving the message of the sermon. The pastor should also prepare to speak the sermon. The following provides a basic sermon template that any pastor can use. The pastor should have a theme for the sermon that gives the main message of the sermon and a clear scriptural passage that communicates the theme.

SCRIPTURE TEXT: The main scripture passage or text that shows the theme of the sermon.

THEME: The main message of the sermon. For clarity, the preacher should be able to state the theme in one sentence.

INTRODUCTION: PRESENT THE PROBLEM ALONG WITH ILLUSTRATION/EXAMPLES

The introduction should present the problem for which the sermon is the answer. It may include illustrations, background of the main scripture passage, and stories or examples. The introduction should be brief.

BODY: The body is the meat of the sermon. To expound the theme of the sermon, the body should have at least three points that are supported by scripture. Each point should connect and naturally flow into each other.

- **POINT #1**: With *scriptural* support
- **POINT #2**: With scriptural support
- **POINT #3**: With scriptural support

CONCLUSION: Summarizes the points of the sermon and emphasizes the theme.

ACTION: Finally, the sermon should have a call to action based on the points of the message. This may be a call to apply it in their lives. It may include an immediate call for repentance or to believe for healing, etc. The minister may ask the congregation to move forward to the church altar to act on the sermon.

BIBLICAL BENEDICTIONS

Numbers 6:24-26 The LORD bless thee, and keep thee: The LORD make his face shine upon thee, and be gracious unto thee: The LORD lift up his countenance upon thee, and give thee peace.

----

1 Corinthians 1:3 Grace *be* unto you, and peace, from God our Father, and *from* the Lord Jesus Christ.

----

2 Corinthians 13:14 The grace of the Lord Jesus Christ, and the love of God, and the communion of the Holy Ghost, *be* with you all. Amen.

Hebrews 13:20-21 Now the God of peace, that brought again from the dead our Lord Jesus, that great shepherd of the sheep, through the blood of the everlasting covenant, Make you perfect in every good work to do his will, working in you that which is wellpleasing in his sight, through Jesus Christ; to whom *be* glory for ever and ever. Amen.

Jude 24-25 Now unto him that is able to keep you from falling, and to present *you* faultless before the presence of his glory with exceeding joy, To the only wise God our Saviour, *be* glory and majesty, dominion and power, both now and ever. Amen.

Revelation 22:21 The grace of our Lord Jesus Christ *be* with you all. Amen.

Philippians 4:7, 20 And the peace of God, which passeth all understanding, shall keep your hearts and minds through Christ Jesus. Now unto God and our Father *be* glory for ever and ever. Amen.

Ephesians 3:20-21 Now unto him that is able to do exceeding abundantly above all that we ask or think, according to the power that worketh in us, Unto him *be* glory in the church by Christ Jesus throughout all ages, world without end. Amen.

It is good for the service to be mixed with the above. Include as many elements of each segment where possible.

3
CREATING A PURPOSEFUL YEARLY PLAN

Pastors should practice making a plan for each coming year. Of course, plans can change as the Spirit leads, but the plan helps to focus for the coming year. It also helps to ensure that the church is fulfilling its purpose. The plan should stem from the vision of the church, and the current strategy that God is revealing. To formulate a yearly plan, let us first review the purpose of the church mentioned in chapter 1.

5 Purposes of the Church

1. Love the Lord with all your heart. Ps 34:3, Matt. 4:10
2. Love your **neighbors** as yourself Eph. 4: 12
3. Go and make disciples Acts 1:8, Matt. 28:19-20. Job 20:21
4. Baptism - baptizing them Eph. 2:19
5. Teaching them to obey Col. 1:28, John 17, Eph. 4: 1-16

A yearly plan should then cover the above aspect. Loving the Lord with all your heart will involve worship. Loving our neighbors involves fellowship and community service. Going and making disciples will include events and activities on evangelism and discipleship. Baptisms and receiving of new members should be a part of our plan. Finally, opportunities to teach believers should be embedded in our plans.

Worship Services

1) Sunday Worship Services
    a. Have multiple services on Sunday
    b. Plan special Sundays such as Youth Sunday, Family & Friends Sunday, New Believers Sunday, Graduation Celebration
    c. Plan for Celebratory Sundays such as Father's Day and Mother's Day.
    d. Mid-Week Services
    e. Revivals and Crusades – geared towards impacting unbelievers and or stirring believers in the church's vision.
    f. Conventions/Convocations
2) Fellowship
    a. Lord's Supper and Washing of the Saints Feet
    b. Youth Fellowship (Services, Activities, Outings)
    c. Other Group Fellowship and Activities (Men, Women, Singles, etc.)

d. Banquet, Prayer Breakfast, Dinners, etc.
   e. Retreats/Camps/ Outings for Different Groups (Youth, Marriage, Whole Church)
3) Community Service
   a. Community Events
   b. Giveaways
   c. Workshops and Seminars
4) Evangelism and Discipleship
   a. Weekly Evangelism Times for the Church
   b. Special Evangelistic Outreach Events
   c. Worldwide Vision Day
   d. New Believers Class
   e. New Believers Day
5) Teaching
   a. Mid-Week Services
   b. Sunday School
   c. Convert Training Classes
   d. Deeper Life Classes
   e. Conferences, Seminars

Knowing the above, keep in mind that the following Biblical events or activities are non-negotiable and should be incorporated into every yearly plan:

1) Frequent Worship and Fellowship Opportunities
2) The Lord's Supper and Washing of the Saints Feet

3) Preaching and Teaching
4) Manifestation of Multiple Spiritual Gifts
5) Offering, Tithes, and Fundraising

The pastor will plan events and activities for the year that covers worship, fellowship, service, evangelism and discipleship, and teaching. Since there are many choices of the types of events that can be planned, the pastoral team should allow the specific vision of the church to guide what events and activities are held. Furthermore, the pastor should seek God for a revelation on an overall theme or strategy to focus on for the coming year. The overall theme or strategy will further guide the year's plan in a specific direction.

So to recap, the pastor would plan for the year by answering the following questions:

- What services and events will we have for worship services, fellowshipping, community service, evangelism and discipleship, and for teaching?
- What is the unique vision of the church that will guide the frequency and types of events?
- What did God reveal as the overall theme or strategy to focus on in the coming year? How does this further fine tune the frequency and types of events for the year?

Now that you have gone through the necessary process for identifying the events and activities that you will have, the next steps are to collaborate with your team, choose dates, and identify the departments, leaders, or committees who will plan and implement the events.

Collaborate with Your Team

At this point, you want to share the overall theme or strategy that God has revealed for the upcoming year. You will let your team know the generic activities that must be covered. At this point you can designate different areas to the pastoral team to further plan out, and then meet together again to finalize. Covering the different purposes of the church, designate the planning of events to your team members based on their gifts and skills. Then, you may meet with the team again to finalize decisions. Alternatively, the planning can be done together in a meeting.

Including your team in the planning produces an early commitment to the success of the events from the leaders. Also, it allows the gifts of the pastoral team to operate in planning the events for the year.

Dating and Timing

The day and time that you will allocate for the events and activities will depend on the Spirit's leading, type of event, customs of your church, and cultural customs of your locality.

The type of event may, at the very least, determine the day that the event will be on. For example, if you have a special a special worship service then it you would most likely designate one of the upcoming Sunday worship services for the event. The question then becomes which Sunday will you have the special service on. The customs of your church and the cultural customs of your locality may help to narrow down the timing. For example, the church body that you are a part of may already have a tradition for the time of year to have the event. It may be best to stick with that tradition. Some events may be determined by the cultural customs of your locality such as Mother's and Father's Day events, school holidays, seasonal changes and such the like.

Maximize Religious Holidays

The wise pastor will maximize Christian holidays such as Easter and Christmas to increase church attendance. Plan special events and activities for the worship services that occur within the time period of these holidays. Put on revival services, crusades, skits, concerts, and such the like during religious holidays. It is a great time to gather as many people out to the church as possible. Study the customs and traditions at your locality to see how the locals may expect church services during Christian holidays.

Take Advantage of Civil Holidays

Beyond religious holidays, there are many civil holidays that the pastor can take advantage of to put on special events. For example, plan youth and community events between the interim that students are out of school and returning. Local customs may involve activities such as feasts, gatherings to eat traditional meals, and similar activities. Churches can host such events and activities as a form of fellowship or even as an evangelistic outreach. Just ensure not to embrace a local custom that is contrary to Biblical teaching. Additionally, civil holidays may be a time to put on revival services if locals are more available during that time.

Build Yearly Expectations

Every church should have yearly events that members and even the community can look forward to and expect. It may be as simple as an annual anniversary service or event. It may be a yearly convention that occurs around the same time each year. A Christmas play or concert may take place at around the same time each year. Members of the church and the community will look forward to these events and invite guests to it.

Create the Plan

Taking all of the above into consideration, it is time to put the yearly plan together. Write out the vision, yearly theme or strategy that God has given on the top of the page. Gather the input from your team and lay out your plan. You can organize the plan by the purpose categories given above or organize by date and state the purpose. You will need to write the name of the event, the date, days, and time. Also, add on the department, leaders, or committee that will plan and implement each event.

Review the Plan

After creating the plan, it is essential to review it. First check to see if the overall plan aligns with the vision and strategy for the church. Secondly, check to see if you have events and activities to cover the different purpose areas of the church. Then, check your dates. You can have an administrator or secretary review the dates and time to avoid conflicts and ensure that the dates are reasonable.

Finally, circulate the plan to your pastoral team and departmental leaders first to get their feedback on potential conflicts and suggestions on areas that may have been missed. Following the review, update the plan as necessary.

Implementing the Plan

Implementing the plan involves ensuring that the departments, leaders, and committees are taking steps to prepare for, promote and execute the events and activities they are responsible for. The pastor can supervise the task of alerting others to begin preparing for the event, or delegate the tasks to someone on the pastoral team.

Additionally, the pastor should have an administrator and secretary regularly check the yearly plan and notify the responsible departments, leaders, and committees to begin preparation as necessary. The pastor should closely oversee the planning of events and activities that will most impact the overall theme or strategy that God has given for that year. Build anticipation and expectation for upcoming events among the members of the church by including them in the planning stages as much as possible from giving them specific items to pray about concerning the event to welcoming them in different stages of the preparation as much as possible.

Remember, change the plan by the leading of the Spirit or as changing needs may arise throughout the year. The Spirit may lead you to postpone, change or cancel an event. There may be changes in the community that create new needs that would require the pastor to implement different events or activities. In a fast-paced, information-rich world, the modern-day pastor must be nimble and ready to formulate different and new activities on the fly.

4
INCREASING THE IMPACT OF YOUR MINISTRY

Every pastor should endeavor to expand the impact of their ministry in their church, community, country, and across the globe. The following are several Biblical points that, when put into practice, will increase the impact of your ministry. Look up, read and study the scriptures that are provided for each point.

- Be Faithful (2 Timothy 1:14)
    - Live a holy life
    - Create boundaries to avoid sin
    - Be loyal to a local church and leadership

- Pray and Fast (Acts 17:21)
    - Pray at least an hour daily
    - Fast at least once per week
    - Fasting can be done from 6 AM to 6PM (or to 3 PM). Complete fasting of food and water is possible for up to three (3) days.
    - Maintain personal health. Consult a doctor if necessary when fasting.
    - Extra time with God in prayer and the Word should take place during fasting.

- Bible Study (2 Timothy 2:15)
    - Prioritize Bible reading, meditation, and study (at least 1 hour daily).
    - Create your own personal outline of the Bible.
    - Create your personal topical Bible
    - Memorize gripping Bible stories (Miracles of Jesus, Acts of Faith, etc.)
    - Memorize gripping Bible verses
    - Memorize Gospel verses
- Expand ministry knowledge and skills (2 Timothy 2:15; 2 Timothy 2:2)
    - Take formal college/seminary courses
    - Read quality Christian books
    - Follow a powerful, mature, and seasoned ministry leader
- Record revelations of your calling to ministry (ex. Paul, Ezekiel, Jeremiah)
    - Memorize associated scriptures with the revelation
    - Refer to it periodically
    - Use it to motivate yourself when you are feeling low
- Covet the best spiritual gifts related to your ministry (I Corinthians 14:1).

- Identify the gifts needed for your ministry (Example: Evangelist – healing and miracles, missionaries – faith, word of wisdom, word of knowledge, deacon/deaconess – helps, mercy, giving).
- Pray for those gifts.
- Exercise the gifts.

- Identify the maximum manifestation of your ministry (Romans 12:6)
  - What effect and impact do you have when operating at the maximum?
  - Ask God to show you the maximum.
  - Endeavor by faith to operate on that level.

- Utilize every opportunity to minister (Acts 20:19-20; Romans 12:11)
  - Minister to others in need.
  - Accept opportunities to exhort, preach, etc.

- Publicize powerful miracles in the ministry (Romans 15:19)
  - Talk about miracles, salvations, healings that occur.
  - Use testimonies of them when ministering.
  - Use it only to glorify God.
  - Write about it.
  - Use it to encourage and build the faith of others.

- Demonstrate the fruits of the ministry.
- Work cooperatively with others in ministry (Example Timothy, Paul, etc.)
  - Submit to leaders
  - Have others join you in ministry endeavors
  - Help others in the ministry
  - Ask for help when needed
- Utilize online media (Isaiah 40:9)
  - Social Media – Facebook, Instagram, twitter, YouTube
  - Upload videos of preaching/ministry
  - Podcast of preaching
- Train others in ministry (2 Timothy 2:2)
  - Teach others how to minister
  - Share your ministry with others
  - Train others to replace you.

Pastors need to teach other leaders around them to enhance their ministry as much as possible for the growth and expansion of the church. Given this, the pastor must understand crucial ministry positions that complement and support the pastoral ministry.

Three ministry positions that potentially provide powerful complements or supports to the pastor are evangelists, missionaries and deacons. The next few pages provide training points for these ministry leaders. Gain knowledge of how evangelists, deacons, and missionaries can perform when operating at their full potential. Also, use this material to develop and motivate the evangelists, missionaries, and deacons assigned to your church.

Training for Evangelists, Missionaries and Deacons

Evangelist

An evangelist is one who brings the "evangel", which is the good news. The evangelist is a messenger of the gospel.

Qualifications of Evangelists (Acts 6:3-8; Acts 8:5, based on Philip the Evangelist)

- Holy Living
- Full of Faith
- Holy Ghost Filled
- Boldness in preaching the Gospel
- Passion to Win the Lost
- Identified and ordained by the presbytery.
- Cooperative with Presbytery

The term "evangelist" occurs three times in the Bible

1. Ephesians 4:11 - listing of ministry gifts
2. Acts 21:8 - Philip the Evangelist

3. 2 Tim. 4:5 - Paul instructing Timothy to do the work of an evangelist

Philip, the Model Evangelist

From the model in the book of Acts, we learn the following about the ministry of the evangelist:

- The evangelist preaches Christ
    - Acts 8:5 Then Philip went down to the city of Samaria, AND PREACHED CHRIST UNTO THEM
    - Acts 8:35 Then Philip opened his mouth, and began at the same scripture, and PREACHED UNTO HIM JESUS.
- Ministry is with supernatural demonstrations (Acts 8:5-8)
    - Miracles and healings will often come with the ministry of the evangelist.
    - Seek God for miraculous demonstrations in the ministry.
- The evangelist's gift works in conjunction with other ministry gifts
    - Acts 8:14 - Peter and John came to minister the Holy Spirit to those who received Christ through Philip's ministry.
    - Be under the leadership of a church body.
    - Works with church leaders to incorporate souls into the church, and church planting.

- In every place of ministry, establish relationships with local church leaders.
- Operates in a Supernatural Traveling Ministry

    Acts 8:4; Acts 8:26; Acts 8:39-40 God even caught away Philip to preach to another city. The Evangelist will receive supernatural <u>Direction</u>, <u>Unction</u>, and <u>Breakthroughs</u> to Preach the Gospel.
    - Create a yearly travel itinerary based on:
        - Leading or burden for different places
        - Requests
        - Need for new church planting
    - Continually raise funds for the ministry. Gain financial support by:
        - Asking for long-term sponsors
        - Having letters asking for support
    - Utilizing funding websites.
    - Be ready for spontaneous trips. Under God, ensure that you are always ready to travel at any moment.

Implications

- Conducts massive soul-winning revivals
    - Two Types: (1) With a local church. (2) With a network of churches or ministries.
    - Plan to use large venues for soul-winning revivals such as parks, auditoriums, stadiums, theaters in collaboration with a network of local churches or ministries.
    - Assist local churches in planning for massive outreach revivals by reaching out to non-members, visitors' list and community through calls, visitations and other forms of follow-up in anticipation of mass revival.
    - Promote the mass revivals - flyers, banners, etc.
    - Build financial support for massive revivals with sponsors and working with local churches.
    - Ensure and assist local churches in having a follow-up/discipleship plan for souls that are saved at the revival.
    - Enlist the cooperation of churches and ministries to pray and fast for the event.
    - Work with and prepare local churches and ministries to have music at the event, lead souls to the altar, minister deliverance during the event.

- Performs strategic outreach
  - Opens the door for church planting in new areas
  - Makes strategic contacts
  - Winning influential people in a community to Christ.
  - Winning people to Christ who opens doors for further ministry in the area.
- Assists in the establishment of churches by:
  - Developing new believers
  - Helping to develop new leaders under guidance from presbytery (Bishops, Overseers, etc.)
  - Strengthening new churches through periodic visits.

Missionary

A missionary is one that is sent - usually sent to a new territory to plant a new church or assists in planting a church. A missionary can also be sent to strengthen existing churches - usually churches that are new. The local church may send a missionary, or the presbytery of leaders may commission a missionary.

Qualifications of Missionaries

- Holy Living
- Holy Ghost Filled
- Bold

- Identified and set apart by presbytery
- Cooperative with Church Body and Leadership
- Passion to Spread the Gospel
- Hardworking

Model: Paul and Barnabas (Acts 13 and 14)

- Brings the Gospel to new or unreached territories for Church Planting (Acts 14:1).
    - Goes to a location as commissioned by the local church or presbytery (Acts 13:1-3).
    - Surveys the area for opportunities to win new believers (Acts 13).
    - Looks for fertile areas (squares, marketplaces, major gathering places, etc.).
    - Conducts house to house evangelism.
    - Connects with recipients already open to the gospel. This includes recipients who are part of the community hoping for a new church plant.
    - Connects with new believers already in the area expecting or requesting a new church plant.
    - Surveys the area for a place to regularly preach the Gospel and teach new believers (auditoriums, halls, hotel rooms, shared space, house etc.). This could include:
        - Asking local community members for possible areas

- - Checking local or neighborhood newspapers and circulation
    - Checking community centers or apartment buildings that can be rented temporarily for a small fee.
    - Checking hotel conference rooms
    - Checking local churches for open space they may be willing to rent
    - Checking for banquet halls and similar venues to rent at times.
  - Builds a directory of available building spaces in the area.
  - Surveys the area for a more long-term place for church services.
  - Works under the direction of the sending church or presbytery to make contact for acquiring building space.
- Remains in an area until the church has the leadership foundations
  - Disciple new converts.
  - Preach and teach as needed.
  - Fill gaps until local leaders are established.
  - Labor in any capacity for the establishment of the church (transportation, sanctuary care, office work, publications, preaching, teaching, etc.).

- - Helps train members for newly assigned positions.
- Periodically revisits to strengthen the churches.
  - Completes tasks assigned by the sending church or presbytery.
  - Generally, strengthens through exhortation, preaching, and teaching.
- Reports to sending church or presbytery of leaders.
  - Regularly reports to sending church or presbytery while on the field
  - Returns to sending church after the task is completed or as directed and provides a full report.

Deacons

Deacons take care of the practical pastoral matters of the church to free the pastor and presbytery leaders to focus more on preaching, teaching, ministering and the spiritual leadership of the congregation. Deacons perform like assistant pastors in the local church.

Deacons are also expected to be strong in the faith, holding to the doctrines of the church, and should be ready to preach.

Qualifications of Deacons (I Timothy 3:8-12)

- Respectable Behavior and Conversation
- Sincerity
- Soberness
- Contentment
- Committed to Sound Doctrine
- Proven
- Disciplined
- Faithful to Spouse
- Good Manager of Household

Practical Duties

Model - Deacons in Acts 6:1-8

- Shepherding
    - Deacon/Deaconess assists the pastor in caring for the congregation through visitations, follow-up with struggling/missing believers, praying for the sick, ministering to bereaved, encouraging and exhorting the saints.
    - Preaching, and exhortations as called upon.
- Administrative
    - Monitoring the general operation of the church - departments, practical matters.
    - Filling gaps in the church's operation as needed.
    - Reporting areas of breakdown to the presbytery

- Care of the Church Facility
  - Ensuring the church property is ready for worship services include opening on time, cleanliness and neatness.
  - Ensure availability of materials necessary for service (bathroom items, baptism items, anointing oil, general envelopes, flyers stocked).
  - Proper and secure closing of church property.
  - Arrange and ensure the maintenance and upgrade of church property (painting, repairs, aesthetics, etc.).
- Benevolence
  - Organizing to assist members in need.
  - Visitations: sick, missing, tragedy-ridden.
- Finances
  - Organize ongoing fund-raising activities.
  - Take up the day-to-day financial burden of the church by sponsoring or raising funds for day-to-day matters.
  - Conserve spending by ensuring that utilities are not misused.

- Logistics
    - Be ready to assist presbytery leadership in a variety of ways - transportation, materials, supplies, items for Lord's Supper, etc.
    - Be ready to fill gaps in a variety of areas where there is a need.
- Events
    - Deacons take care of the practical matters to prepare for major events such as upgrading and improving the facilities.
    - Help to plan for events.to

Keep in mind that to increase the impact of your ministry begins with your spiritual devotion, and diligence in using your spiritual gifts. But it also involves developing and training others working with you. The above overview of deacons, evangelists, and missionary tasks is to get you started in training others.

5
FOSTERING AN EVANGELISTIC CHURCH

The great commission to preach the gospel to every creature is the responsibility of every church. A growing church will seek to win souls to Christ. The goal is for the body of Christ to increase in number, not to cycle Christians from church to church. So, how can a pastor foster an evangelistic church? First, the pastoral leaders of the church must embrace the Biblical mandate for every member of their church to spread the gospel and win souls. The following is clear from the Word of God.

1. God calls every Christian to be a witness and a preacher of the gospel (not a pulpit preacher, but a gospel preacher) Acts 1:8, Matthew 4:19.
2. Early Church Example (Acts 8:1-4)
3. In the early church all the believers shared the gospel.
4. Evangelism Continual in Life
   - Christ at the well John 4
   - Philip with Nathanael (john 1)
   - Peter at the Temple Gate (Acts

- Paul in Jail (Acts 16:22-34)

Evangelism is more than just an event; it should be our way of life

Secondly, pastors and ministry leaders should equip members to witness, preach, and share the gospel (Ephesians 4:11-12). Pastors and ministry leaders should be the coach, and the believers should be on the frontline.

Best as On the Job Training

The best way to get members to be evangelistic is for the pastoral team to do evangelistic work. Evangelism is best caught than taught. Beyond teaching evangelism in a class, we must also train believers to learn while evangelizing with other mature believers.

Therefore, pastoral leaders should first be the examples by going out on the streets, in the marketplaces, in the community to share the gospel, and motivating church members to come along.

The pastoral team can develop a regular time for evangelism such as once per week. The pastor and the church can partner with other ministries and movements in having a regular time of evangelism. Worldwide Vision Day is a worldwide movement where believers from different churches and ministries unite worldwide in preaching and witnessing on the same day, on the first Saturday of every three months, or every quarter (Find out more at www.worldwidevisionday.org). There are also other evangelistic movements around the world.

The pastoral team should consider it a priority to raise up soul-winners, given the importance of winning souls to Christ. It is important that believers are trained to win souls to multiply the amount of people to be saved.

Mass Recruitment

Pastors should recruit the entire church to evangelize by preaching on evangelism and inviting the congregation to preach and witness in the community. In addition, the pastor should highlight evangelistic efforts by allowing active members to testify and report on the number of souls coming to Christ.

Individual Invitation

In addition to mass recruitment, the pastor, and ministerial team should invite members of the church on an individual basis to join them in winning souls just like Jesus did with the disciples.

Here is the cycle that should take place:

1. First, the pastor invites members.
2. Trained or experienced members and leaders invite other members to join.

3. Trained and experienced members train other members with on-the-job training (demonstrating as they do it).

Strategy for Raising Up Soul-Winners

- Enlist Prayer Warriors
    - Committed believers who are not yet committed evangelists.
    - Ask the prayer warrior to pray alongside you while you preach and witness.
- Recruit Trainers

Encourage ministry leaders and experienced soul-winners in the church to find other believers in the local church to give them on-the-job training during evangelism efforts. The following are some examples of church members to target to be trained:

Characteristics of Members to Select for On the Job Training

- Faithful Christians
- Willing
- Teachable
- Young People - (that exhibit the above qualities).
- Married Couples - (that exhibit the above qualities).
- Men and women - both can preach and witness.

- New Believers - usually hungry to share Christ.
• Conduct Teachings or Classes on Evangelism

While this should not replace training while actually evangelizing, it can be beneficial. The following information topics should be covered:
- Evangelism Scriptures
- Handling Common Objections to Salvation
- Basic Witnessing Approach
- Leading a person into accepting Christ
- How to Preach
- How to Share Personal Testimony
- How to Give Next Step Instructions to a New Believer
- Preparation for persecution and attacks

• Organize Evangelistic Teams
- Motivate every to preach the gospel.
- Organize teams to reach certain locations.
- Select a leader for each team.
- Give the opportunity for teams to give public reports on their evangelistic efforts.

Teaching Believers to Share the Gospel

1. Have them memorize a simple Gospel Presentation Outline
2. Have them memorize gripping Gospel Scriptures
3. Have them learn some illustrations that can be used.

4. Encourage them to make it their own.

6
BASIC DISCIPLESHIP TRAINING

Winning souls to Christ is great, but pastoral teams must be skilled in developing a new believer to maturity. Discipleship is necessary so that new believers become fruitful members of the church, and not just attendees. This chapter gives the foundational steps for leading a new believer into maturity. Pastors can also teach committed members of the church so that they are involved in the work of discipling new believers.

INITIAL STEPS AFTER SALVATION (WHEN A NEW BELIEVER FIRST COMES TO CHRIST):

1. Pray for the new convert (I Thess. 3:10)
2. Written Correspondence - given to new believer. Examples: Letters, cards, newsletters. The church office will send letters.
3. Telephone/Virtual Meeting
    - Call should be made within 24 hours
    - Be brief and friendly
    - Smile while speaking to the person.

- Call again on the day before the next main service, preferably by another person.

4. Give Growth Gifts

    - Example: certificates for converts class/topic completion, scripture keys, pamphlets, DVD's, website links, books, etc.

5. Visit - First Visitation

    - It is best for the first visit to be within the first 7 days of the new believer's Christian life. During the first 7 days, a discipleship team member should set an appointment for visitation.
    - Given recent technological advancements, a virtual meeting can also be set up with the new believer.

Crucial Actions During Visit or Virtual Meeting:

- Introduction

    - Introduce discipleship team to new convert.
    - Ask about their week.
    - Ask about or discuss their last visit to church

- Testimony - have a team member share his/her testimony.

- Give Assurance of Salvation
    - Assure them of their salvation - that they are forgiven; that they are children of God. Teach them to walk in it by faith and not depend on their feelings. Give them the assurance that if they sin, their salvation is not over, but that they can confess their sins to Christ, and continue to walk in the cleansing of His blood.
- Growth

Ask if they are practicing the things that are crucial to their growth:

- Bible Reading and Study
- Prayer
- Church Attendance
- Witnessing
- Follow up on previous assignments, gifts, etc. that were previously given/discussed.

- Pray with them.
- Teach, focusing on the "How", Not Why.
    - How to Pray
    - How to Testify
    - How to Study the Bible
    - How to Fast
    - How to Witness
    - How to Overcome Temptation
    - What to Do if They Sin

BASIC NEEDS OF A CONVERT

- Assurance–knowing that they are saved.
- Acceptance–knowing that they belong to the family of God.
- Protection–from all spiritual threats to their growth in Christ, such as false religions, false doctrines, accusers, persecutors (2 Cor 13:7)
- Fellowship–with the saints
- Food–the Word of God (I Peter 2:2-3)
- Training
- Instruction on the main ingredients for Christian living (I Thess. 2:11)

Addressing the Needs:

Assurance

Teach the new convert about what has taken place in his new walk with God:

- Review the Gospel message with them.
- Ask them to tell you how they know that they are born-again.
- What it means to be born again?
- Share your testimony and introduce them to the testimony of others.
- Observe how they share their conversion experience with others.

- Share Biblical examples of conversion.
- Emphasize that there is a change in attitude toward Christ and sin (I John 1:1-9) Emphasize that change in behavior will involve a process (I John 2:1-3; Romans 12:1-2; 2 Peter 1).

Acceptance

- Show love for them.
- Work hard for their spiritual growth.
- Show concern for their well-being.
- Pray for them.

Protection

- Personally, pray against any attack on their Christian life.
- Organize a prayer team to pray for them.
- Ground them in the word.
- Warn them of dangers
    - False doctrines and teachings
    - Former friends and family persecution, accusation, and pressure
    - Remaining in guilt because of sin

Fellowship

- Connect them with strong Christians in their age group.
- Connect them with the other members of the church.

- Overlook minor faults in the early stages of their walk to build fellowship.
- Ensure they receive constant encouragement. Hebrews 3:13 tells us to encourage one another daily. Look at other one-another scriptures for instructions to apply to the treatment of new believers. (Ephesians 4:32, Colossians 3;13, John 13:34, Romans 12:10).

Food

- Teach them the word.
- Teach them how to feed themselves.
- Instruct them on studying the Bible.
- Instruct them to memorize the Word.
- Instruct them to study the Bible on their own consistently.

Hearing the Word (Prov. 28:9; Jer. 22:29; Luke 19:28)

- Take convert to church with you.
- Teach convert how to take notes. Share with him how taking notes is a blessing for you.
- Share with him the blessings of the sermon to your life.
- Encourage him to share how the message impacted him with you and others.
- Give him preaching DVD's, or suggest videos, podcasts online, etc.

The Bible (2 Tim 3:16-17; 2 Peter 1:21; Matt 22:29; Psalm 19:7-11; Psalm 119:105)

- Help the convert in getting a Bible. Teach him the dangers of some translations.
- Show him how to use a concordance.
- Show him how to use cross-references, marginal notes, and other study Bible tools.

Reading the Word (I Tim 4:13; Revelation 1:3; Deut. 17:19)

- Share your own blessings from personal Bible reading.
- Read a section of the Bible with the convert.
- Motivate him by getting him started reading a new testament book for example St. John.

Scripture Memorization (Col 3:16; Matt. 4:4)

Share the blessings of scripture memorization from personal experience and Biblical examples.

- Memorize a verse together.
- Review verses together.
- Check on how he is doing.
- Connect with others who are memorizing scripture.
- Provide a scripture memory tool for him.

Bible Study (Acts 17:11; Prov. 2:1-5; Ezra 7:10)

- Share with him the benefits of Bible study.
- Do an actual Bible study with him.

- Show him the difference between study and reading.
- Give him personal Bible study methods to use.

Meditating on Scripture (Psalm 1; Joshua 1:8; Phil 4:8)

- Share a blessing from personal experience.
- Meditate aloud. Go through a passage with him, while sharing with him how you think on the passage.
- Teach him how to. Tell him to ask questions of the passage such as "who, where, why, how". Think about the main points of the passage and how it applies to your life. Tell him to depend on the Holy Spirit for illumination.
- Share with him a meditation plan

Bible Study Methods

New converts can learn basic Bible study methods. Other Bible study methods, such as biographical study, word study, book background study, and survey study, may be too advanced for the new convert. Note that believers have access to online Bible study websites such as Bible.cc and Biblegateway.com. The following study methods are appropriate for the new convert.

- Devotional—read a short passage and then meditate on it for application in your own life.

This is an essential first step Bible study method for teaching new converts. Ask the following questions as you read:

- What does this passage say to me?
- Where am I falling short?
- Give specific examples.
- What am I going to do about it?

Take notes of your reflection for future reference.

- Thematic Study

This is another method to teach a new convert following the devotional method. The convert will need a study Bible and an exhaustive concordance, or use a Bible study website such as Bible.cc or Biblegateway.com.

- Choose a theme, one that helps you solve a personal problem, answer a question, strengthen a weakness.
- Find verses on the topic using a concordance; use verses that directly relates to the theme.
- Ask questions to yourself about what each verse says about the topic.
- Apply it to your life.

- Chapter Summary
  - Read a chapter in its entirety.
  - Give a caption to describe the chapter.
  - List the major points of the chapter.

- List the major characters in the chapter.
  - Key verse or verses
  - keywords
  - Difficulties or misunderstandings
  - Use cross references in your Bible to help you understand it.
  - How is Christ revealed in the chapter?
  - What are the major lessons of the chapter?
  - Apply the findings to your own life.
- Topical Bible Study

The convert will need to have a study Bible, exhaustive concordance, and possibly a topical Bible.

  - Decide on a topic and list all the words related to the topic.
  - Read and study every verse related to the topic.
  - Compare and group the verses you have studied.
  - Create an outline of your results.

Training

- Focus on "how to", not why (I Thess. 4:1)
- Be an example —Model how to do things (Phil 4:9)

Do "How to" Training

- How to Pray
- How to Testify
- How to study the Bible

- How to share your faith
- How to memorize scripture
- How to overcome temptation
- How to overcome persecution

Remember that the goal of discipleship is for the disciple to become fully functioning mature believers. The disciple should grow to a point where he or she is winning souls to Christ and discipling them to maturity also. Discipleship cannot just be done in classes; instead, the discipler must be a model for the disciple. Use the information in this chapter to disciple new believers in your church and to teach your workers how to disciple new believers.

6
MINISTERING DELIVERANCE EFFECTIVELY

Evil spirits exist and work to destroy people's lives spiritually, emotionally and physically. Demonic spirits often work to divide families, and will even seek to bring division in a church. The equipped pastor will know how to minister deliverance to those who are experiencing demonic oppression, and how to conduct spiritual warfare. Counseling alone may not be sufficient to handle some spiritual bondages. Therefore, the pastor should be ready to minister deliverance to members and congregants in the church.

This chapter first begins with preparing yourself and then goes into general steps for ministering deliverance. This serves as a guide; the pastor should be sensitive to the Holy Spirit's leading in order to minister deliverance effectively. Jesus empowered his disciples to cast out demons and to heal the sick. The same anointing from Christ works through us today to minister deliverance to those who are oppressed. Therefore, pastors should be prepared.

Self-Preparation

- Strong Prayer Life
  - Through prayer God may reveal hidden things about the person in bondage.
  - **Fasting and Prayer** (Matt. 17:21; Mark 9:29).
  - The faith to cast out certain demonic spirits only comes through fasting and prayer.

- Clean Heart
  - Love
  - Humility and submissiveness (remove pride)
  - Purity

- The Whole Armor of God (Ephesians 6:12-17)
- Know Demon-Busting/Deliverance Scriptures
  - Luke 10:19; Mark 16:17; Col. 2:15; Rev. 1:18; Matt. 16:19; I John 4:4; Phil 2:10-11.

- Watch Your Own Spirit
  - Ensure that your spirit remain strong with the word and prayer.
  - Remove all impurity of mind and spirit (II Cor. 7:1).
  - Follow your "spiritual intuition" (conscience) as long as it is in submission to the Word and the Holy Spirit (Rom. 9 :1).
  - Pray in the Spirit (speaking in tongues).

- Develop a Balanced Understanding of satan's power
    - Satan is a defeated foe (Matt. 12:22-29; I John 3:1-10; Matt. 28:18; Eph 1:19-23; Phil 2:9-11; I Pet 3:22)
    - Believers have been delivered and given power over the enemy (Acts 10:38; Eph. 4:8; 2 Cor. 4:3-6; Col. 1:12-14; Heb 2:14-18; Rom 16:20; 2 Cor. 2:11; 2 Cor 10:3-5; Eph 2:6; 3:10; 6:10-20; Col. 2:8-15; James 4:7-8; I Pet 5:8-11; I John 2:12-14 5:18-19; Rev. 12:11)
    - However, satan can take advantage of believers if we are ignorant of his devices (2 Cor. 11:2-4). A believer's mind can be deceived like Eve.
- Exercise Spiritual Warfare
    - **Personal Level** - Self-Deliverance: learning to submit to God, resisting the devil and casting demons out of our own lives is the first exercise in spiritual warfare. If we cannot do this, our spirits are unprepared to deal with more difficult levels of spiritual warfare.
    - **Pastoral Level**
        - Begins with ministering deliverance to family members, friends, etc.
        - Extends into regular ministry in a local church.

- **Evangelistic/World Level**
    - Strategically coming against territorial spirits, and spirits over regions.
    - Engaged in ministering deliverance in different parts of the world.

Deliverance Team

Pastors can select a team of workers who are effective in ministering deliverance. It may be the pastoral team and other leaders in the church that are proven in having authority over demonic spirits.

- The deliverance team should comprise of proven believers who are living a godly life.
- The team members should have a life of prayer and regular fasting.
- Team members should be in prayer while the leader is ministering deliverance.
- Team members should be discerning to assist the leader as needed.
- A team can be anywhere from three to six people.

Pre-Counseling

As the Holy Spirit leads, it is often beneficial to speak with the candidate needing deliverance before ministering to them. Pre-counseling may provide information that you will need to minister deliverance effectively. It also ensures that the candidate is willing to receive deliverance.

- Instruct the deliveree what to expect.
- Instruct the person what sins have been keeping him or her in bondage. Dr. Ed Murphy calls these "sin handles" (Murphy 2003) (Eph. 4:27)
- The person needs to repent of all sin.
- Instruction that obedience to the Word of God will be necessary for total deliverance.
- Instruct the person to reject the conclusion and lies that keep him or her in bondage.
- Gather information about the person's life. This can help reveal areas of demonic invasion in the person's life.
    - What are the "sin handles" that need to be repented of.
    - Has the person been involved or associated with the occult, witchcraft, horoscope, psychic consultation, or any kind of divination?
    - Generational or familial sins that need to be renounced. (Example: family involved in the occult, witchcraft, idol-worship. Or, the head of the family is committed to a sinful practice and passes it through the family, such as prostitution, business crimes, palm reading, worshipping ancestors, etc.).

- Was the person a victim of some physical, emotional, mental, or sexual abuse?
- Is there any kind of substance abuse?
- Instruct the person on what to do after being delivered: (1) Getting filled up with the Word of God (2) Regular fellowship (3) Regular prayer life.

Post - Deliverance Counseling

After the deliverance session, it will be necessary to provide further instruction to the deliveree.

- Post - Deliverance Counseling is necessary in order to discover all the "sin handles" in the person's life.
- The deliveree needs teaching and counseling to recognize the devil's tactics to put him or her back into bondage.
- The person may have other areas of demonic attachment in his/her life that will need to be exposed.
- There may be major character flaws in the person's life. Therefore, the person will need teaching on walking in godliness.
- Those who have been abused physically, emotionally, or sexually may need further counseling for total healing.
- Teach the person how to deliver themselves.

The Deliverance Session

- Begin with a pre-counseling session. Even a short session is better than none.
- Make sure the deliverance team members are prepared.
- Cover any innocent bystanders under the blood of Jesus Christ if in a public place.
- You may begin with a short prayer to God. (Cover bystanders, yourself, deliverance team).
- Instruct the deliveree to renounce all divination connections, occult involvement, etc.
- Instruct deliveree to repent of all sins.
- Break all curses over the person's life as led by the Holy Spirit or if you are already aware of curses in the person's life.
- Cast out all demonic spirits. Use the scriptures as you cast out the demons. If you know the name of the spirit in operation you can cast it out by name using the pertinent scriptures to address it.
- If there is resistance, and the spirit do not leave, check for the following:
    - Is there any occult jewelry on the person that needs to be removed?
    - Is there any area that the person needs to let go of such as forgiving someone, renouncing a divination or occult involvement, etc.

- If a person refuses to let go of an area, then end the session, and counsel the person further.

Legal and Safety Considerations

For safety and legal reasons be mindful of the length of deliverance sessions, the presence of others, the amount of physical exertion, the health condition of the deliveree, and the age of the deliveree. It is strongly recommended that pastors and church leaders research the legal liabilities that they may face in their locality, or consult professional legal experts. The tips presented in this book are basic considerations, and not a replacement for legal counsel.

Ministering to Young Children

When ministering to young children at about the age of twelve or under, be calm and ensure that parents are at the deliverance session. In fact, have the consent and presence of parents for any age group legally considered minors in your locality. When ministering to children, you will need to ask parents questions that would help in ministering to the child. When ministering to a boy with a dumb and deaf spirit, Jesus questioned the father about the boy's condition (Mark 9:20-25). Additionally, it may be necessary to counsel or even minister to the parents also (Mark 9:22-23).

Consider the Crowd

Furthermore, Jesus also considered the presence of others when ministering deliverance. So it may be wise to lessen the time, or change the location of a deliverance session to avoid undue attention from others who may not understand. Concerning the boy with the dumb and deaf spirit, Jesus quickly commanded the devil to leave the child "when Jesus saw that the people came running together" (Mark 9:25). At other times, when the unclean spirit would speak out, Jesus would command it to stop speaking (Mark 4:32-35, Luke 4:41). Consider ending a deliverance session and continuing at a later time if it is causing undue attention from innocent or ignorant bystanders. Alternatively, the deliverance session may be moved to a different location.

Generally, it may be necessary to limit the time of a deliverance session. Both the deliverer and the deliveree may be exhausted from a session. Remember that a deliverance session can be continued at a different day or time. Furthermore, when a deliverance session is taking place in a public area such as during a church service, it is unwise to consume a majority of the time to minister to one person. Questions and disputes arose from the crowd when the disciples of Christ were unsuccessful in casting out the dumb and deaf spirit from the young boy. Unwanted attention was drawn to the situation as the disciples probably attempted multiple times to cast out the spirit (Mark 9:14-19).

Be Careful with Physical Exertion

Physical exertion may occur during a deliverance session because of the demonic activity or because of the need to assist the deliveree. If the deliveree has been weakened, disabled or wounded by the demonic spirit, assistance may be needed. For example, Jesus asked for the boy with the dumb and deaf spirit to be brought to him (Mark 9:19). The dumb and deaf spirit threw the boy to the floor (Mark 9:20). Therefore, someone on the deliverance team may need to help by holding or lifting a person to move them and or prevent them from harming themselves or others.

However, physical exertion should be kept to a minimum and may not even be necessary. Only do this where assistance is needed. Otherwise casting out the devil with a command or rebuke is sufficient (Matthew 17:18, Mark 5:8, Luke 4:35-36).

Repeating for emphasis, take extreme precaution to avoid causing harm when assisting the deliveree. Those assisting should consider the amount of physical pressure being placed on the deliveree and end or reduce the physical exertion as necessary. Additionally, be mindful of the deliveree's health issues that may affect their breathing and their strength. Stop a deliverance session whenever someone's health may seem at risk.

Other Health Considerations

Considering legal ramifications, do not recommend or utilize deliverance as a replacement for treating medically diagnosed conditions. For example, conditions such as seizures, asthma, epilepsy, brain injury and other ailments that may cause convulsions will need medical attention. Furthermore, some mental problems arise from medical conditions such as dementia, delirium, amnesia and other similar ailments. Those with such medical conditions would need medical attention. This is not to downplay the power of prayer and deliverance, but rather to recognize the need for accountability with medical professionals recognized by civil authorities.

We have power over demonic spirits through the Lord Jesus Christ (Luke 10:19). God has also anointed us to minister healing to the physically, emotionally, and mentally sick (Isaiah 61:1). Therefore, pastors and ministry leaders can minister deliverance with confidence knowing that the power of God will manifest to set people free.

7
TIPS ON PASTORAL COUNSELING

Contrary to what some may believe, counseling is not the main task of the pastor. Preaching, teaching, and spiritual leadership are the main tasks of the pastor. However, counseling is necessary as a part of pastoral work. The pastor should avoid leading by counseling. Instead, preaching, teaching, and providing spiritual care for the congregation should be the primary ways to lead the church. Counsel only as necessary.

Certain members of the pastoral team, and other leaders of the church may be gifted counselors. Delegate counseling needs to other leaders of the church where possible. Take the following into consideration when delegating and assigning leaders to counsel others:

- There must be clear evidence that the leader has applied the Word of God to overcome challenging situations in their own life.
- The relationship the leader may have with the person or congregants – A leader who may already have a trusting relationship with a parishioner may be best suited to counsel them.

- The sex of a leader. Sometimes, it may be best for ladies to counsel other ladies, and males to counsel other males.
- The role of the leader: it may be best for a leader to counsel those within the domain of their department. For example, the youth pastor may be best suited to counsel the young people, or the leader of the men's department may be best for counseling the men, etc.

The following are some of the areas where counseling is vital and necessary:

- Premarital Counseling
- Marriage Counseling
- Family, Relationship, and Interpersonal Conflicts
- Major Life Decisions – career, school, finances, relocation, etc.
- Calling to Ministry
- Grieving a Loss
- Pre-Deliverance Counseling – guiding a person into what to do for freedom from a sinful habit or a demonic bondage.
- Post-Deliverance Counseling – necessary guidance and instruction for someone who has just been delivered from demonic bondage.

There is a need for counseling when parishioners need guidance in applying the scripture to the situation. The pastor only provides Biblical counseling. In situations where the Bible is clear, its best for the pastor to avoid prolonged counseling sessions for such matters, and exhort the parishioner to obey God's Word. However, there may be current situations in a person's life where they may need a pastor's insight and guidance to apply the wisdom of God's Word to the situation; this is where counseling is necessary. Otherwise, preach and teach the Word of God.

Biblical Counseling

Biblical counseling is guiding people towards doing God's will in personal, social, mental, and spiritual matters using the principles taught in the Word of God. Therefore, it is crucial that the counselor knows the Word of God and has ample experience in applying God's Word to a variety of situations. The counselor must be proven. The fruits of God's Word can be seen in their life in a variety of situations.

Biblical Counseling is NOT:

- Providing professional information and instruction – the pastor should not try to be a doctor, lawyer, financial manager, etc. when counseling. Even in situations where the pastor may have professional knowledge, the pastor should still avoid providing professional instruction in order to avoid personal liability.

Instead, the pastor shares the wisdom of God's Word concerning the matter and allow the person to decide what to do.
- Always giving one direct solution – the pastor must be ready to lay out options for the person based on the principles of God's Word, and let the counselee decide what to do.
- Shaming the person into action – the pastor is not seeking to make the person feel guilty in order to act or make a change. However, the pastor should depend on the Holy Spirit to convict the counselee during the counseling process so that the counselee will decide to turn from their sin.

What Biblical Counseling is

- Guiding the person towards seeing the insights of God's Word to their situation. The key is that the counselee will see for themselves through God's Word the actions they need to take.
- Revealing the counselee's spiritual condition using the Word of God. The pastor leads the counselee through God's Word regarding their actions and behavior so that they see for themselves, the errors in their actions.
- Providing a Biblical perspective on the person's challenges and situations. This may include leading the person to see God's promises in the situation the counselee may be facing.

- Providing prophetic insight on the decisions and actions that the counselee may take. This is showing the counselee through God's Word what will take place if they act in one way or the other.

Tools for the Counselor

Now knowing what counseling is, let us discuss the tools that the counselor needs. First, the counselor will need a thorough, complete knowledge of God's Word. Knowing the necessary areas where counseling is usually needed, the counselor must gain a comprehensive understanding on what the Bible teaches on the following topics: marriage, relationships, interpersonal conflicts, family conflicts – these may include anger, malice, bitterness, parenting, offences, unforgiveness, care, love, fruits of the Spirit, etc.; making decisions, the will of God, hearing God's voice, knowing the call of God; deliverance, freedom from bondage, remaining free, etc.; grief, death, recovering from grief, life, resurrection. The counselor may need to read books on the topics.

Other tools the counselor needs are the spiritual gifts that would be of great help for counseling such as the gift of prophecy, word of wisdom, the word of knowledge, and discerning of spirits. These are revelation gifts that will give the counselor supernatural wisdom for a situation (word of wisdom), knowledge previously unknown (word of knowledge), and seeing the spirits at work (discerning of spirits). With the gift of prophecy, the Holy Spirit gives a message to speak to admonish, encourage, or comfort the hearers (1 Corinthians 14:3).

What Not to Do in a Counseling Session

- Guide the person before fully understanding the situation.

- Provide general cliché answers to the person's problem.

- Instruct a person on matters that may require professional or diligent research.

- Give the counselee the impression that you are the all-knowing answer to their problem.

- Accuse other people that the person may bring up during the session.

- Focus the counseling session on discussing others instead of guiding the counselee.

- Allow the counseling time to become a venting or gossiping session.

- Promise the person one hundred percent confidentiality. We will further discuss why this cannot be promised.

Confidentiality

While the pastor should do his best to keep the counselee's issues totally confidential, he cannot promise this in a pastoral context. The Bible teaches us that a witness may need to be brought in when a believer has sinned or caused an offense. In addition, the Bible teaches that the matter should be brought to the church if a person continues in sin (Matthew 18:15-17). Therefore, the pastor should endeavor to keep the issues of the counselee from spreading or causing public shame, but he or she cannot promise total confidentiality. Of course, it is a sin for the pastor to gossip, spread rumors, or indiscreetly share secrets with others. Furthermore, to build trust, the pastor must demonstrate that he can be confidential. However, the pastor should communicate where total confidentiality is not possible. Often, the pastor may be able to keep the matter completely confidential, but he cannot promise this.

In all cases, it is best that the minister relays to the counselee that he may need to share the issue with at least one other minister, or trusted leader in the church. Being able to share the matter with at least one person is for the pastor's own protection. Furthermore, the pastor should communicate to the counselee that if they continue in an immoral sin, the matter may need to be brought to the entire pastoral team, or board of trustees.

In the following cases, the pastor may not be able to keep a counselee's issue totally confidential: confessions of intention to hurt someone or to hurt oneself; confessions to a felony or a serious crime that the pastor is required to report; confessions of recent sexual or physical abuse; continuation in immorality that may require church discipline; other matters of church discipline that may involve other ministers and church leaders; situations involving a minor that must be shared with parents; and any matter that would cause harm to the counselee, counselor, others, or the church. In essence, given the circumstances, pastors may have to reveal things communicated during a counseling session to the church's leaders, to civil authorities, and to family members.

All that being said, the pastor must do his or her best to keep matters from counseling sessions confidential. The counselee should have some assurance that the pastor will be confidential as much as possible, and will only reveal a matter where absolutely necessary.

Legal Considerations

Increasingly, churches are facing legal liability in the area of counseling. Following the tips in this chapter may help to minimize these liabilities. However, every church should diligently research the local laws in their locality and take the necessary precautions as necessary. Officially, only use ordained ministers to provide Biblical counseling, as they may be less exposed to liability when giving religious advice.

It is strongly recommended that pastors and church leaders research the legal liabilities that they may face in their locality, or consult professional legal experts. The tips presented in this book are basic considerations, and not a replacement for legal counsel. Below, you will see some of the main legal liabilities that churches may face.

Types of Legal Liabilities

Negligent Counseling - churches have been held liable for providing advice that goes beyond Biblical instruction. Be careful to only provide Biblical advice. Give the Biblical principles on the issues, and leave the personal life decisions up to the counselee.

Sexual Abuse – avoid accusations of sexual abuse by counseling with at least one witness in the room or in close proximity. Counselors should only be ministers that have a strong reputation of fidelity in their marriage and relationships.

Breach of Confidentiality – churches can be held liable for failing to guard the private information of people being counselled (personal, health, family info). Keep all personal matters confidential. A good practice is to have a consent agreement outlining what can and cannot be kept confidential.

Failure to Disclose or Intervene – failing to report matters that must be reported by law. As stated before, the minister cannot promise total confidentiality as some criminal matters would need to be reported. Again, having a consent agreement is advisable.

Example Pastoral Counseling Consent & Release Form

Please read through this Consent & Release form, which outlines the expectations for the Biblical counseling that will be provided.

Counseling
We only provide Biblical counseling. Biblical counseling will guide you to face the challenges of life to the glory of God through the teachings of the Word of God. We do not provide secular psychology, psychiatry, or therapy. The pastoral leaders counsel from Biblical teachings, but they do not practice psychiatry or psychotherapy. The pastors also do not provide medical, financial, or legal advice. Only counseling on Biblical principles is provided. The pastoral counselor and you, the counselee, have the right to end a counseling session at any time for any reason without any moral or legal obligations.

Confidentiality
It is understood that all statements in your pastoral counseling sessions are confidential and will not be disclosed. However, for certain situations, the law and/or our church practices may require that certain information be revealed without your consent. Confidentiality is waived in the following circumstances.

1. Pastors reserve the right to consult with and share matters from a counseling session with at least one other pastor or minister.
2. Matters of physical or sexual abuse may need to be reported to the proper authorities.
3. We may need to disclose to the appropriate person, agency, or civil authority any harm that a person may attempt or desire to do to one's self or others.
4. In the cases where a person knowingly and consistently refuses to repent of a sinful practice, it may be necessary to bring the matter to other leaders and parishioners of the church. (Proverbs 15:22; 24:11; Matthew 18:15-20).
5. We reserve the right to share any matter when compelled by the civil authorities for issues of a criminal nature.

Security and Church Workers
There may be a church worker present or in close proximity during a counseling session for security and assistance. They are expected to keep any matter that they may hear confidential.

Waiver of Liability
In your understanding of receiving Biblical counseling from a pastor or ministerial leader, you agree to release and waive any and all claims of any kind against the church or its ministers and workers arising from or relaying to participation in pastoral counseling.

Agreement
I have read the above Counseling Consent & Release form. I accept these policies and agree to proceed with biblical counseling.

Print name here: _____
Signature: _____ Date: _____

What to Do in a Counseling Session

- Pray before starting the counseling session. In fact, the pastoral counseling session should lead the counselee to look to God and go to Him for help.
- Tell the person what to expect. Let the person know that you only provide counseling through the Word of God.
- Get informed consent from the counselee. The counselee should agree to your statement on confidentiality whether by signing a statement or verbally agreeing to your statement. Generally, let the person know that you will do your best to keep the session confidential, except for sharing it with at least one other minister or church leader. However, sometimes you may need to share the matter (See the section above on confidentiality).
- Listen carefully to the counselee. Try to hear the counselee's perspective, motives, confessions, accusations, and Biblical understanding on the matter.
- Ask questions. Ask questions to clarify the counselee's perspective, motives, confessions, accusations, and spiritual understanding on the matter.
- Repeat key things that the counselee stated to ensure that you fully understood what they shared. Ensure you have all the necessary information

before proceeding to applying scriptures or ministering to the person.

- Use appropriate scriptures that specifically address the counselee's situation. Use the scriptures to show God's perspective on the matter, letting the counselee see for themselves the difference with their perspective. Let the Word of God reveal their motives whether good or bad. Minister to any confession of sin using the principles of God's Word. Lovingly correct any Biblical or spiritual misunderstanding.

- Share a story as led by the Spirit. It may be a Biblical story, a testimony you may be aware of, or a personal story that is appropriate to share. Sometimes a person may be able to identify with a story and gain a new perspective.

- Take accusations seriously but do not join in the accusation. Instead, Biblically share what steps the counselee should take to resolve the conflict with that person. Strongly discourage the person from spreading the accusation, but instead to follow the Biblical process.

- Minister to the person as led by the Holy Spirit. In some cases, you may need to minister deliverance. If the person recognizes their sin as you shared appropriate scriptures with them, you may assist the person into a prayer of repentance.

- For matters that are not specifically addressed in the Bible, provide scriptures that gives the principles that the counselee should follow. The counselee may need to weigh their options, do further research, gather more information, or wait on God for answer. In these cases, avoid telling the person what to do, and instead share the Biblical principles that should be applied, and allow the counselee to make the final decision.

- Give the person an assignment to complete to help them with their issue. The assignment may be to read a scriptural passage, resolve a conflict with a person, research a matter, or complete a task. Some counseling session, such as premarital counseling, may involve multiple session with assignments between sessions.

- Equip the counselee with resources as necessary. Recommend books and even give a book as a gift or temporary loan. Recommend an expert for a matter where you may not have the answer (i.e., medical, financial, or legal expert).

- In all sessions, always close in prayer.

Limitations and Boundaries

Counseling can be draining and even detrimental, if the pastor does not establish certain limits and boundaries. For counseling sessions, the pastor should limit the times, locations, and persons.

Set Appointments

Where possible, the pastor should avoid spontaneous counseling sessions. Pastors often minister to others spontaneously as led by the Spirit. However, for situations, where an in-depth counseling session is necessary, the pastor should practice having parishioners set an appointment. Even in a ministering situation, where it is clear that the deliveree may need more in-depth counseling, the pastor should give short immediate instructions and schedule a counseling session later. Establishing a procedure of setting appointments will help the pastor from being overrun with counseling tasks. Furthermore, it provides further accountability and protection for the pastor, as he can make these appointments known to his spouse, family, and other church leaders and workers.

Often, counseling can extend beyond one session. Marriage counseling may often involve more than one session. For ongoing counseling sessions, set clear times and dates. Give assignments to the counselees; this helps to reduce the length of the counseling sessions.

Limit the Locations

Usually, it is best to have the counseling session at an appropriate place in the local church. Ensure that there are others at the church during the counseling session both as witnesses and for personal protection. If possible, meet in an area where others can see you. If this is not possible, you can have someone sit or stand by the office door or room with the door cracked open.

In most cases, it is unwise to go to the counselee's home to conduct a counseling session. If you go to someone's home, you may not know what situation you are stepping into. Definitely avoid going to the home of the opposite sex alone as this is ripe for accusation and sexual temptation. If you must go to someone's home, then take someone with you. Inform the counselee that if you must come to their home, then at least one other person will be with you.

If you must meet with someone outside of the church, it should be a public place within view while having a private conversation. If necessary, have other church leaders or workers to be in the area. Ensure that the place is safe.

Virtual meetings have become popular. Keep in mind that if you meet with someone virtually, it is crucial not to meet alone. In virtual settings, people may say or do inappropriate things. A witness helps to avoid false accusations. Additionally, be aware that the session may be secretly recorded so be careful what you say.

Limit the Persons

Most pastors are compassionate and so willing to meet with anyone. However, the pastor should have limitations on who to meet with. Family members, and close friends may not be the best people to counsel as you may be less objective in these situations. Recommend family members and close friends to another minister as necessary.

Be careful when having counseling sessions with the opposite sex. It is best to have a witness in these situations, either having someone in the room with you or in close proximity. For some sensitive matters, recommend someone of the opposite sex to a church leader of the same sex. Do not be afraid to end a counseling session and recommend someone to another minister or church leader as necessary.

The pastor is not under any obligation to meet with someone. Pastors can avoid meeting with any person with whom they may feel uncomfortable. When a person is setting an appointment, it may be beneficial to find out the general counseling topic; if the pastor feels uncomfortable dealing with that topic with the individual, the pastor is free to recommend the person to someone else. Similarly, a pastor should end ongoing counseling sessions that seem unproductive or counterproductive.

Counseling is not the main task of the pastor, but a necessary work. Pastors must counsel under the Spirit's guidance and with diligence. Finally, counseling is a form of spiritual ministry to the counselee, and not a medical, psychological, or therapeutic practice.

8
MINISTERING THE BAPTISM OF THE SPIRIT

It is crucial that pastors preach and teach on the baptism of the Holy Spirit to build the faith of the people to receive. The baptism of the Holy Spirit can occur at any time without a specific time to minister the Spirit.

Ministers should listen to the leading of the Holy Spirit. While we can minister the Spirit by faith, with the leading of the Spirit, the anointing flows freely for the candidate to receive and speak in other tongues.

1. Begin with Faith

Galatians 3:5 He therefore that ministereth to you the Spirit, and worketh miracles among you, doeth he it by the works of the law, or by the hearing of faith?

Build your faith in the fact that God gives the gift of the Spirit freely to all true believers. Internalize the following scriptures to build your faith:

- It is a distinct promise of the last days - Joel 2:28.
- It is universal promise to the Body of Christ - Luke 11:13; John 7:37-39.

- Available for generations to come - Acts 2:39.
- Available to as many as the Lord would call - Acts 2:39.
- Baptized in the Spirit — Acts 1:5; 11:16; Matthew 3:11; Mark 1:8; Luke 3:16; John 1:33.
- The Spirit coming, or falling, upon — Acts 1:8; 8:16; 10:44; 11:15; 19:6; Luke 1:35; 3:22.
- The Spirit poured out — Acts 2:17,18; 10:45.
- The gift my Father promised — Acts 1:4.
- The gift of the Spirit — Acts 2:38; 10:45; 11:17.
- The gift of God — Acts 8:20; 11:17; 15:8.
- Receiving the Spirit— Acts 8:15,17,19; 19:2.
- Filled with the Spirit— Acts 2:4; 9:17; also, Luke 1:15,41,67.

Prayer should build the minister's faith to minister the baptism of the Holy Spirit including regular times of speaking in tongues, fasting, and internalizing words of faith.

2. Increase the Faith of the Candidate

Acts 19:2 He said unto them, Have ye received the Holy Ghost since ye believed? And they said unto him, We have not so much as heard whether there be any Holy Ghost.

Instruct the candidates for the baptism of the Holy Spirit that it is a freely given gift:

Quick Teaching to Build Faith:

- **Spirit in You.** Upon salvation, the Spirit of God dwells within you for conviction, spiritual growth, and assurance of salvation. John 4:14 *But whosoever drinketh of the water that I shall give him shall never thirst; but the water that I shall give him shall be in him a well of water springing up into everlasting life.* John 14:17 *Even the Spirit of truth; whom the world cannot receive, because it seeth him not, neither knoweth him: but ye know him; for he dwelleth with you, and shall be in you.* I Cor. 3:16 *Know ye not that ye are the temple of God, and that the Spirit of God dwelleth in you?*
- **Spirit Upon You.** The same Spirit in you comes upon you to empower you for service - this is the baptism of the Holy Spirit. It is the same Spirit filling you up and overflowing upon you. Therefore, there is no need to be afraid or think the Spirit's baptism is difficult to receive, since the Spirit is already in you, and the same Spirit will come upon you to empower you.

Joel 2:28 I will **pour out my spirit upon** *all flesh; and your sons and your daughters shall prophesy*

Acts 1:8 But ye shall receive power, after that the Holy Ghost is **come upon you**:

- Utterance in Tongues

    When the Spirit comes upon you, initially, the manifestation of the power is with speaking in tongues. Acts 2:4; Acts 19:6; Acts 10:44

3. Pray

Build an atmosphere of prayer and praise in expectation of the outpouring of the Spirit.

Acts 8:15 Who, when they were come down, prayed for them, that they might receive the Holy Ghost:

Acts 1:14 These all continued with one accord in prayer and supplication, with the women, and Mary the mother of Jesus, and with his brethren.

Instruct the Candidate to Pray (1) Repent of any Sin (2) Ask for the Baptism of the Spirit

4. Lay Hands on the Candidate

Acts 19:6 And when Paul had laid his hands upon them, the Holy Ghost came on them; and they spake with tongues, and prophesied.

Release your faith as you lay hands. You can lay hands by simply placing one of your hands on the head of the candidate.

5. Speak

In faith, speak, for example, "Receive the Holy Spirit" over the candidate. Expect the candidate to receive and speak in other tongues.

Acts 9:17 And Ananias went his way, and entered into the house; and putting his hands on him said, Brother Saul, the Lord, even Jesus, that appeared unto thee in the way as thou camest, hath sent me, that thou mightest receive thy sight, and be filled with the Holy Ghost.

As you lay hands, speak by faith in Jesus that the person receives the Spirit.

6. Encourage (Acts 10:44-48)
- Worship with the person
- Do nothing to hinder or discourage
- Be a witness

7. Instruct

Instruct the candidates not to be afraid, but to speak in tongues as the Spirit gives the utterance Acts 8:14; Acts 19:1-7.

Build a prayerful atmosphere in the church, where members seek after God, and the manifestation of his power. In a prayer-filled, praise-filled atmosphere, the Holy Spirit will move freely. Encourage the manifestation of the gifts of the Spirit with prophetic utterances, speaking in tongues, revelations, gifts of healing and so on. In this atmosphere, new believers will quickly be baptized in the Spirit.

9
BECOMING A PROPHETIC CHURCH

MOBILIZE THE PEW TO PREACH THE GOSPEL

The local church that is consistently engaged in winning the lost through gospel preaching and personal evangelism are ready to receive from the Spirit of Prophecy. The testimony of Jesus is the Spirit of Prophecy. Pastors and church leaders should activate their congregation to regularly preach and witness on the streets and from house to house in their city.

PROPHESY THE WORD OF GOD

The Bible is prophetic. Pastors and church leaders that prophetically expound on the Word of God are training their congregation to have prophetic insight. There are several ways pastors and church leaders can prophesy using the Word of God.

1. Use the Bible to prophesy on societal and governmental sins.

2. Prophesy future prophecies of scripture. Train the congregation to recognize and share with others the calamities and behaviors happening today that were clearly prophesied in scripture.

PARTNER WITH A PROPHET/PROPHETIC CHURCH

1 Samuel 10:10 And when they came thither to the hill, behold, a company of prophets met him; and the Spirit of God came upon him, and he prophesied among them

The prophetic anointing is transferable. In the Old Testament, the Spirit of Prophecy would come upon those who would join a company of prophets.

Therefore, a church can begin to operate in the prophetic by partnering with a prophetic ministry or church. Allow a proven, godly living prophet to minister to the congregation. Be careful to ensure that the prophet is proven by the accurate fulfillment of multiple prophecies and evidence of a godly living lifestyle. Partner with any godly living minister of the gospel who faithfully preaches the Word of God and often operates in the gift of prophecy and prophetic revelation with accurate fulfillment. Furthermore, fellowship with churches that demonstrate evidence of the prophetic manifesting in their midst. Highlight the prophecies and fulfillments that are given by true prophets. Take the time to publicly speak prophecies that a proven prophetic ministry or church releases. Then highlight the fulfillment of the prophecy when it occurs.

MINISTER THE BAPTISM OF THE SPIRIT

Some assemblies no longer emphasize or encourage the baptism of the Spirit with the evidence of speaking in tongues. However, the outpouring of the Spirit upon the church brings the unction to prophesy as spoken of in Joel 2:28.

ENCOURAGE MEMBERS TO SEEK FOR THE GIFT OF PROPHECY

1 Corinthians 14:1 Follow after charity, and desire spiritual gifts, but rather that ye may prophesy

Church leaders should teach the importance of the gift of prophecy, and the scriptural instruction to desire and seek for its manifestation. This is a direct teaching from the Bible.

EXPECT PROPHETIC UTTERANCE

While praying for the manifestation of the gift of prophecy, there should be an expectation of faith that prophetic utterances and revelations will begin to manifest in the church. Therefore, encourage members to prophesy and acknowledge when a prophecy is from the Lord.

Encourage the people to write down revelations, dreams, visions, word of knowledge, etc., that they receive from the Lord and share it with the pastoral team. Publicly speak those prophetic revelations that have been tested and are clearly from the Lord.

MAINTAIN ORDER

As the faith of a church rises in expectation of the manifestation of prophecy, prophetic utterance and revelation will take place. Several members in the church may begin to speak aloud in prophetic utterance in the church, and more will present their prophetic revelations. While this is happening, the ministerial leaders of the church must diligently endeavor to maintain order while not quenching the prophetic fervor in the congregation.

During worship services, depending on the size and composition of the church, generally, one person speaks at a time while someone records to evaluate and republish the prophecy. All others should listen and assess the prophetic utterance. Two or three may speak at the same time if this can happen without confusion, and a group of witnesses can hear each one. Again, someone should be designated to record the utterances of each person so that it can be further evaluated and possibly republished. Huge churches may need to train ministerial teams to listen to and record prophecies in the congregation at appropriate times. Otherwise, the utterer can privately share the message with a ministerial leader without disrupting the order of service. The goal is to encourage the manifestation of the gift while maintaining order.

Before publicizing or acting on them, ministerial leaders, or an appointed team should first evaluate the prophetic revelations, dreams, and visions of lay prophets in the church. Pastoral leaders should ensure that revelations that are spoken to the church or acted upon have been vetted for accuracy.

DEVELOP A PROCESS FOR JUDGING REVELATIONS

Implement a process of discerning and interpreting dreams and revelations based upon the following Biblical principles.

1. Do not despise prophecies. Encourage leaders and congregants to share their prophetic utterances and revelations, including dreams, visions, word of knowledge, etc. While testing all things, do not quench the gift.
2. Reject anything that undermines the deity and humanity of Christ. Any form of revelation that

denies, even in part, that Jesus Christ is fully God and fully man should be rejected.

3. Reject anything unbiblical or carnal.

4. Create a team of those gifted in interpretation, discernment, and prophecy who will judge prophecies and revelations that are given.

5. The team should prayerfully look over and evaluate revelations.

6. Evaluate the life and character of the person giving the revelation or prophecy.

    a. Are they committed to the local church and its leadership?

    b. Have they demonstrated fruits of godly living or repentance?

    c. Are their teachings and doctrines Biblical?

    d. Have they previously given a prophecy or revelation that came to pass?

7. Evaluate the credibility and necessity of the prophecy or revelation.

    a. Is it Biblically aligned? Reject anything that violates any command or teaching of scripture.

b. Are there any confirmations, leading, or prompting from the Spirit that it is from God?

c. What impact will it have? For example, will it build up or destroy a church? A "revelation" that would be destructive or divisive may not be from God. However, some revelations may be from God but should not be released publicly but handled discretely.

d. What is the purpose? The purpose may be to bring warning, to edify, to comfort, to correct, to glorify God, to confirm, to ignite, to mobilize, etc. When unable to determine a purpose, it may be best to rest the revelation until receiving further clarity.

8. Only publish prophecies and revelations that are proven and sure. A prophecy may be from God, but if the team is unsure, keep it unpublished and ask the Lord to give further clarity. God will often reveal the matter in a different way or through someone else. The responsibility of the church is to apply the command of scripture to evaluate the prophecy.

RECOGNIZE PROVEN PROPHETS IN THE CHURCH

The pastoral leadership should recognize the prophetic office on faithful leaders and members who consistently prophesy with accurate fulfillments and preach the truth.

Often God will confirm the ministry of the prophet in a local church by using him or her to give multiple strategic prophetic revelations and utterances for the development of the church. Or the Lord may give the person numerous revelations concerning events in the nation or around the world with accurate fulfillments. Therefore, leaders will clearly see the need for the ministry of that prophet in the assembly.

The leaders can publicly acknowledge the gift in the person through a declaration and a formal ordination. Moreover, local congregations may connect with a prophetic ministry for the public appointment of the person to the ministry office of the prophet.

EXALT JESUS CHRIST EXCLUSIVELY

Revelation 19:10 I fell at his feet to worship him. And he said unto me, See thou do it not: I am thy fellowservant, and of thy brethren that have the testimony of Jesus: worship God: for the testimony of Jesus is the spirit of prophecy.

While you acknowledge proven prophets, the glory must remain on Christ. Fulfilled prophecies should be publicly acknowledged so that God is glorified in all things. Strictly avoid the exaltation of any man whom God mightily uses in prophecy.

The prophetic revelations and utterances are from the Lord through the Holy Spirit. We are only his servants. Ensure that all praise goes to Him (2 Corinthians 12:7-10).

GUARD AGAINST FALSE PROPHECY

Avoid giving space to anyone who claims to be a prophet but is unproven in character and reputation.

Avoid giving space to any type of claimed prophecy or revelation that engineers rebellion and slander of local church leaders, and fuels backbiting and gossiping.

Give no room to the spirit of divination. The spirit of divination acts as a counterfeit form of prophecy. Any form of revelation that comes through consulting the dead, palm reading, psychic readings, horoscopes, astrology, etc. are from the devil. Some churches invite the spirit of divination through incense burning, old testament ritualism, and unbiblical sacraments.

Jeremiah 23:28 The prophet that hath a dream, let him tell a dream; and he that hath my word, let him speak my word faithfully. What is the chaff to the wheat? saith the LORD

THE PROCESS AT HARVEST ARMY CHURCH INTERNATIONAL

Since the late twentieth century, the Harvest Army Church has been prophesying of events to come upon the earth. However, from 2004 with the ninth (9th) hour revelation, a multiplied number of prophecies have been given through the ministry. Leaders and members of the church alike have given many prophetic revelations over the years that all come to pass. The Chief Presiding Bishop of the church body often states that the main actions of the church are fasting and praying, preaching the gospel, and living a holy life. The following is the process that the church follows to evaluate and publish prophetic utterances and revelations.

Encouragement of members to operate in the gift.

A team is appointed to evaluate. A selected team of mature and proven workers has access to read over and check the prophecies and revelations.

The team evaluates the lay prophets' prophecies. The selected team members assess the prophecies and decide if they are from God or not. This decision is made based on the known character and the reputation of the person submitting the prophecy. The person's character is evaluated based on the person's integrity, manner of life, commitment to a local church body, and accountability to local church leadership. Evaluation of the person's reputation has to do with the accuracy of past prophetic utterances and revelations given by the person, and whether the person's teachings and doctrines are Biblically sound. If a person may be a new or unknown believer, the leaders or team will seek a confirmation from the Spirit of God.

Each utterance or revelation is scrutinized. Finally, even with a proven reputation, we determine if each submitted utterance or revelation is from God. If we are unsure, we leave the prophecy alone and wait for further revelation from God. Our decision is based on Biblical alignment, the witness of the Spirit, and whether the given utterance or revelation has any purpose. For example, we often reject predictions of the identity of the next United States' president during the election season since such prophecies have little to no spiritual edification and rarely glorifies God.

Interpretation of the prophecy as needed. Often, we ask the lay prophet to state their interpretation of the revelation. Secondly, those with the gift to interpret dreams and visions will give their insight. Interpretation is made prayerfully. Correct interpretation only comes supernaturally.
Publication. Often in groups of three, we publicly announce the revelations and prophecies. The prophecy is also publicly released in written form online. Only prophecies and revelations that are sure will be distributed.

The process at the Harvest Army Church International is based on the instructions of 1 Corinthians 14 along with the general Biblical understanding of God's working in revelations. Every church looking to be prophetic will need to develop a similar process based on God's Word to ensure order.

9
OFFICIATING A WEDDING

GENERAL CONSIDERATIONS

Depending on the bride and groom's wishes and the culture's practices, the wedding can have many different components. For example, singing is a part of many weddings and possibly even short speeches from family, friends, etc., to the bride and groom.

Whenever possible, marriage officiants should include other ministers to pray, read scripture, and even share a short ministerial message on marriage. Some couples may want to write their own vows. As a Christian minister, you may request to review their vows to ensure that it is Biblically aligned.

PREMARITAL COUNSELING

It's highly recommended that before agreeing to officiate a marriage, the minister should ensure that the engaged couple has gone through a reasonable amount of premarital counseling. Premarital counseling will ensure that the couple understands the Biblical mandate of marriage, the responsibilities and roles of the husband and wife in marriage, and the Biblical instructions for building a healthy marriage.

While ministers should encourage new marriages, premarital counseling can help individuals to avoid marrying the wrong person or entering marriage unprepared.

Premarital counseling should be Biblically-based, with practical advice. The following are suggested topics that should be covered: (a) Spiritual, Emotional, Financial Preparedness for Marriage (Are You Ready for Marriage?) (b) Determining Spiritual and Emotional Compatibility (Should you Marry this Person?) (c) Changes that Occur with Marriage (d) Roles of the Husband and the Wife (e) Financial Care and Stability (f) Threats to a Healthy Marriage (g) Blessings of Marriage (h) Vision and Goals for the Marriage Union (I) Sexual Intimacy.

THE WEDDING CEREMONY

Despite the differences in wedding ceremonies, all weddings should include the following basic components.

Some examples below are from "The Broadman Minister's Manual" by Franklin M. Segler (1969). It is beneficial to every minister to have a minister's manual as a resource for conducting various types of services and sacraments.

1. Open in prayer
2. Read Scripture - (Example: Ephesians 5:25-33)
3. Opening words of the Officiant

Example:

Dearly Beloved, we are gathered here today in the presence of these witnesses, to join (insert groom and bride's names) in matrimony. Marriage is honorable among all; and therefore, is not to be entered lightly but reverently, passionately, lovingly and solemnly. Into this - these two persons present now come to be joined.

4. Giving of the Bride
5. Ask: Who gives the bride to be married?
6. Comment on Marriage / Sermon
7. **Question to Bride and Groom** (Answer with I Do) - Have them hold right hands

Minister to Groom: ____ (insert name) _____ do you take __ (insert name) _____ to be your wife. (Other comments can be made here as to the commitment of the groom to the bride)

(Groom says I Do).

Minister to Bride: ____ (insert name) __ do you take __ (insert name) _____ to be your husband. (Other comments can be made here as to the commitment of the bride to the groom) (Bride says I Do).

8. Exchange of Vows

    (say to groom/bride repeat after me)

    I, (Bride/Groom), take you (Bride/Groom), to be my (wife/husband), to have and to hold from this day forward, for better or for worse, for richer, for poorer, in sickness and in health, to love and to cherish; from this day forward until death do us part.

9. Exchange of Rings
    - Comment on what the ring represents.
    - Example Comment: The ring symbolizes the lifelong bond that you are entering into as you exchange vows. Your vow to each other can be honorably broken in the sight of God only by death. As a token of your vows, you will give and receive the rings.

    Minister to Groom: You will give the ring and repeat after me:

    (name of bride) With this ring I pledge my life and love to you, in the name of Jesus Christ our Lord.

    Minister to Bride: You will give the ring and repeat after me:

(name of husband___) With this ring I pledge my life and love to you, in the name of Jesus Christ our Lord.

1. Prayer for the Couple

After the prayer, the legal signing may be done now before the final declaration of the marriage.

2. Declaration of Marriage

"By the power vested in me as a minister of the Gospel of Jesus Christ, and by the laws of the State, I now pronounce you husband and wife. "What God has Joined Together, Let No Man Put Asunder". You may now kiss the bride.

3. Introduction of Newlyweds

"I present to you Mr./ Mrs. and Mrs. / Mr. (insert name) "

While the minister, or the couple, may add other in the ceremony, the basic elements above are necessary. Ministers should check the local laws in the province where the marriage ceremony will take place and follow the procedures necessary to have a legally binding marriage.

10
CONDUCTING THE LORD'S SUPPER

Jesus instituted the Lord's Supper. The Bible teaches us to do it as often as possible in remembrance of Him (1 Corinthians 11:23-26).

The Lord's Supper should be done sacredly. Ministers should ensure congregants have a solemn understanding of the Lord's Supper and its meaning. The Lord's Supper is in commemoration of the Lord's body and His blood. While partaking, participants should reflect on what the Lord's sacrifice has done, and how we are now one as partakers together in Christ.

PRELIMINARIES

The pastor may appoint the ministerial leadership, deacon board, or the mother's board, to prepare the bread/wafer, and the grape juice for the Lord's supper. They should also prepare the necessary cups and serving plates.

Ministerial leaders or deacons can be chosen to serve the bread and the drink during the ceremony. The pastor should communicate to the servers the order in which the serving will be done. The congregation may be served first, and then the pastoral leaders (or other varieties)

SUGGESTED ORDER

1. The Lord's Supper ceremony may begin with a song as the pastor is led.
2. Scripture Reading: read a scripture on the Lord's Supper. The following scripture can be used: (1 Corinthians 11:23-32).
3. Short Sermon or Exhortation on the Sacredness of the Lord's Supper
4. Reflection: Give the congregation the opportunity to reflect on partaking in the Lord's Supper, examine themselves and repent of any sins.
5. Partaking of the Bread
   - It may begin by reading the Scripture in Matthew 26:26 And as they were eating, Jesus took bread, and blessed it, and brake it, and gave it to the disciples, and said, Take, eat; this is my body.
   - Prayer: Following Jesus' example, pray with a blessing for the bread and for the grace given through Christ's sacrifice to manifest fully in the saints.

- Serving of the Bread: A ministerial team, board of deacons, or a mother's board can serve the bread. It may be served to the congregants first, then the ministers, or the ministers first, then the congregants. The pastor should determine the order beforehand and share it with the servers.
- Eating of the Bread: In Jesus' own words, the pastor may say, 'As Jesus said', "Take, eat, this is my body. You may now eat."
- Singing: The Praise and Worship Team may sing an appropriate song concerning Christ's sacrifice on the cross.

6. Partaking of the Drink

    - Scripture Reading Continued.: Matthew 26:27-28 And he took the cup, and gave thanks, and gave it to them, saying, Drink ye all of it; For this is my blood of the new testament, which is shed for many for the remission of sins.
    - Prayer: Giving thanks for Christ's shed blood and its significance in the life of the saints.
    - Serving of the Drink: The same team or a different team from the bread servers can serve the drink. Again, the servers may be ministers, deacons, or the mother. It may be served to the congregants first, then the ministers, or the ministers first, then the congregants. The pastor should determine the order beforehand

and share it with the servers. Drinking: In Jesus' own words, the pastor leads the congregation by saying, "drink ye all of it".
- o Singing: The Praise and Worship Team may sing an appropriate song concerning Christ's shed blood.
- o Altar Ministry: This may be an opportunity to pray for the sick and other areas of need. In remembrance of Christ's body and blood, raise the people's faith to receive wholeness in every part of their lives and minister to them as led by the Holy Spirit.

Remember that the Lord's Supper is a solemn event. It is when we memorialize Christ's sacrifice on the cross. Participants should partake in the supper with reverence. As such, give all believers the opportunity to partake or abstain, and give sufficient time for self-evaluation and repentance.

11
WASHING OF THE SAINTS' FEET

We observe the washing of the saints' feet from the example Christ had set. The washing of the saints' feet exemplifies humility and servanthood.

Usually, the washing of the saints' feet is observed following the Lord's Supper, but it can be done at any designated time.

PRELIMINARIES

The pastor should designate the deacon board, mother's board, or lady's auxiliary to make the necessary preparation for the washing of the saints' feet. Several washing basins will be needed to accommodate the size of the congregation. There also needs to be sufficient towels to dry each foot that is washed. Basins with water should be prepared prior to the feet washing with enough towels to distribute. Designate separate areas for males and females. Foot-washing should be done between members of the same gender (male or female), to avoid awkward or inappropriate situations.

A distribution team will need to be ready to distribute the basins and towels at the set time, collect and refill basins with water as necessary, and give out more towels as needed.

During the washing of the saints' feet, avoid forcing or pushing guilt on anyone who may feel uncomfortable in participating. Rather, allow an open door for all believers to take part, and the freedom for anyone to decline. The pastor should ensure that all leaders are aware of allowing the freedom to participate or not applying pressure.

SUGGESTED ORDER

1. Scripture Reading: John 13:1-15
2. Short sermon or exhortation as to the meaning and the example that Jesus set in washing the disciples' feet. The pastor can preach on themes of humility and servanthood as led by the Spirit
3. Prayer
4. Direction: The pastor may direct the congregants as to the area they will sit for the washing of the feet. Direct the men to the designated area and the women to the designated area. The designated team should distribute the basins and towels. The pastor may designate if leaders and those on the distribution team should wash first or after the congregants.

5. Example: The pastor may be first to wash another's feet as an example and to demonstrate servanthood as Jesus did.
6. Washing of Feet: Congregants take turn washing each other's feet.
7. Singing: During the foot washing, the Praise and Worship team may sing songs with themes of servanthood, humility, Christian service, and foot washing.
8. Testimonies - members may share their testimonies on the blessings of serving God and others.
9. Closing Prayer and Benediction.

The washing of the saints' feet reminds us of the need to serve each other, and to walk in humility. Our Lord gave it as an example, and it was practiced in the early church (1 Timothy 5:10). Therefore, it is a wonderful ceremony for the church to practice today.

12
PERFORMING BAPTISMS

GENERAL CONSIDERATIONS

Baptism is a Biblical command. In the early church, baptism was done immediately after a person came to Christ. Biblically, baptism is an immediate act following salvation. There is no scriptural basis to delay baptism since it is an act of faith and obedience.

Every church should make the preparations to be ready to baptize a new believer. The church should have the following:

- A Baptism Pool (or easy access to a large body of water). Ensure the baptism pool is clean and ready for each church service with a proper water temperature.
- New baptismal clothing for the candidate
    - Preferably, gowns for women
    - Shower caps or similar hair protectant covering for women
    - Large towels
    - Shirts
    - Sweatpants or similar pants for men
    - New undergarments

- o Slippers
- o The baptismal clothes should be new and or fully cleaned and sanitized after use. Gowns, shirts, pants, and towels can be cleaned and sanitized, and reused if they are in good condition. Undergarments can only be used once. Slippers can be cleaned and reused.

- Room or available space in the bathroom for candidates to change.

ADMINISTERING BAPTISM

1. Timing: Baptism should be done immediately or as soon as possible after a person confesses faith in Christ.

    - o After a person has come to Christ at an altar call, have a counseling team of ministers /evangelists/ deacons ready to motivate and counsel the person to get baptized. While not applying any pressure or force, the minister should use the scriptures to convince the candidate of the necessary step of baptism.
    - o Ministers should be ready to baptize the person once they are willing.
    - o Team should be ready to guide the candidate to the baptism location. Provide baptism garments if the candidate did not bring his/her own.

- Carefully guide the person into the water and advise him/her for safety.

2. Prayer: The minister performing the baptism or another minister should pray over the water.
3. Confession of Faith: If deemed necessary, ask the candidate to confess faith in Christ. The minister may also ask the candidate if they have surrendered his/her life to Christ.
4. Directions: Instruct the candidate to clasp his/her hands together (like having hands together to pray). Instruct the candidate to use his/her hands to cover the nose as he/she is immersed into the pool.
5. Position: The minister should position himself next to and slightly behind the candidate to immerse the candidate easily.
6. Baptize: Perform baptisms in shallow water (knee deep). There should be another person (minister, deacon or strong member) present to support the baptizer and for safety reasons.
    - The baptizing minister should place one of his hands on the base of the candidate's neck between the shoulders and hold the hands of the candidate with the other hand.
    - Then before performing the baptism, the minister should repeat the following (or something similar):

Upon the authority vested in me as a minister of the Gospel of Jesus Christ, and upon your confession of faith in Jesus Christ as Lord, I now baptize (insert candidate's name) in the name of the Father, of the Son, and of the Holy Spirit.

- The minister will then lower the candidate into the water until the face of the candidate is slightly below the water and then raise up the candidate out of the water into an upright position. The minister may need to move forward slightly or bend to keep balance based on the relative body size of the candidate.

7. Praise and Testimonial: You may allow the candidate to reflect, praise God or even testify as they wish. Joyous singing can also take place. The congregation may join in worshipping God for the baptism of the new candidate.

8. Direction out of the water: Direct the candidate out of the water (pool etc.). Those on the baptismal team can assist the candidate to exit safely. Provide a towel and slippers to the candidate as necessary. Next, guide the candidate to the changing area.

9. Post-Counseling: After the baptism, and the candidate has changed, further instructions should be given to the candidate to continue in the

faith. Provide new believer materials to the candidate. Instruct the baptized believer on the benefits of regular church attendance, daily prayer, daily Bible reading, and testifying and sharing the gospel with others. Instruct the candidate on attending new convert's classes. At least one person should be assigned to the new believer to disciple them in the faith.

Again, baptism is a Biblical command. Every church should take the proper care to be ready to perform baptisms regularly and safely. It is the duty of pastoral leaders to teach the congregation, especially new believers, of the importance and necessity of water baptism.

13

PERFORMING FUNERALS

GENERAL GUIDELINES

Upon hearing of a death, the minister should visit the deceased's family as soon as possible. If visitation is not possible, the minister should send a message of condolences or speak to the family by phone as soon as possible.

When visiting the family of the deceased, praying, and sharing scripture with condolences are sufficient. It is unnecessary to say many things. Instead, listen to the family as they grieve and offer comfort with your presence and compassion.

At the appropriate time, make arrangements for the funeral with the family. The minister or those appointed from the church may aid the family with the program as much as possible. Include the family in the funeral program. Of course, the minister should insist on the spiritual standards of the service and reserve certain aspects of the program for ministerial leadership. While the family is included, the minister should maintain the solemnness of the service.

The pastor or minister may include other ministers and church leaders in the program such as to moderate the service, pray, read scriptures, lead in singing, etc.

SUGGESTED ORDER OF SERVICE

1. Processional. Usually, the ministers enter before the casket (unless the casket is already placed ahead of time). The congregation should stand as the ministers enter.
2. Statement on Purpose of Gathering and Condolences to the Family: Unless the minister knew the person well as a member or leader in the church, comments on the person's life should be kept to a minimum.
3. Opening Prayer
4. Scripture Reading (Examples: Psalm 90; John 14:27; Psalm 23; 1 Thessalonians 4:13-18; 1 Corinthians 15:19-22; Revelation 21:1-7)
5. Hymn/congregational singing or special singing
6. Reflection: Either chosen by the family as part of the program and can include anyone willing to share – limit the time if reflection is open to anyone.
7. Eulogy
8. Special song/congregational singing of hymnal.

9. Sermon: With the reality of death facing the audience, the sermon is an opportunity to present the hope of the Gospel.
10. Closing Prayer
11. Last Viewing
12. Instruction for Final Processional

THE GRAVESIDE SERVICE

1. Prayer
2. Scripture Reading (Example: Revelation 1:17-18; John 14:19; Revelation 14:13; 1 Corinthians 15:51-57; John 14:1-3)
3. Committal of Body to the Ground:

   o This body we commit to the ground *(to its resting place)*, ashes to ashes, dust to dust.
4. Prayer for the Family
5. Singing

Even after the funeral, leaders should follow up with the family to offer support and comfort as they grieve.

Christians have the hope of everlasting life in Christ. Therefore, it is best to treat funerals of faithful believers like a homecoming. The believer has gone on to be with the Lord.

14
BABY DEDICATION

PRE-CONSIDERATIONS

The baby dedication is not a baptism. The baby is not receiving salvation. For salvation, a person needs to consciously accept Christ at the age of understanding before being baptized. Baptism always follows repentance and faith.

During baby dedications, parents acknowledge the need for God's blessing upon the child and the grace for raising the child in the fear of the Lord. The parents present the child in the Lord's care as they commit to nurturing the child in God's will. The minister lays hand upon the child pronouncing blessings for the child's well-being and prayer for the godly raising of the child.

PRELIMINARIES

The church's administrative office should collect the necessary information regarding the parents, child, Godparents, and family for record-keeping and present a Certificate of Dedication. Many families may wish to dress the baby in commemorative attire for the dedication (such as all-white dress or suit); the family may also do the same. However, there is no requirement for a specific form of dressing for the dedication ceremony. Any formal attire appropriate for a church service is suitable enough for the dedication.

SUGGESTED ORDER

1. The minister will begin by stating that he will conduct the dedication, and request the family, relatives and witnesses to approach the altar.

2. Song: The congregation, led by the Praise and Worship team, may sing a song related to the dedication. The traditional hymn, "When Mothers of Salem" is a good choice. However, there are other songs that are appropriate for dedication.

3. Scripture Reading: The minister will read a scripture that demonstrates the act of baby dedication (for example Matt 19:13-15).

4. Short Message: The minister can make a few remarks that explains the dedication, its importance, and the parents', family members' and Godparents' responsibility.

5. Anointing of the Baby: The minister takes the baby in his hand. The minister or an associated minister anoints the baby with anointing oil

typically on the forehead in the name of the Father, Son, and Holy Spirit.

6. Prayer for the Baby: The minister then prays for the baby's general well-being and growth in wisdom, knowledge, and the fear of God. The prayer should include asking God for wisdom and grace for the parents to raise the child in the fear of God.

7. Declaration of Dedication: The minister declares the baby dedicated. For example: *Upon the authority vested in me as a minister of the Gospel of Jesus Christ, I now dedicate (insert baby's name) in the name of the Father, Son, and the Holy Spirit.*

Jesus was glad when children were brought to him for a blessings. Similarly, pastoral leaders should encourage baby dedication in their local churches. The pronouncement of blessings upon the child with the laying on of hands releases favor into the life of the child.

15
CONDUCTING A GENERAL MEMBER'S MEETING

A general member's meeting includes all the official members of the local church. For best practice, do not promote the meeting to non-members since the general public may not understand the internal issues of the meeting. Additionally, only members can vote on matters.

A member's meeting will include part or all of the following:

- For the pastoral leaders to share the plans and strategic direction of the church.
- Reports from the departments in the church, including upcoming plans or goals.
- Provide information to members on the state of the church finances and budget for the future.
- Nomination and or voting for department positions and local officer's board.
- Clarify, correct or fine-tune protocols and procedures for the worship service and the general and departmental activities.

- State and announce appointments by the senior pastor and Officer's Board of leadership changes, department members, etc.
- Answer questions and concerns from members.

Example Agenda

- Prayer and Scripture Reading
- Welcome, Presentation of Agenda, and Statement of Norms and Procedures for the Meeting.
- Pastoral Report and Strategic Plans. This includes report of the church's growth, general health, and growth plans.
- Reports from Departmental Leaders. Reports include accomplishments from the past year and plans for the future.
- Appointment of members. pastoral appointments and voting on nominees.
- Financial Report of the Past Year. The financial or administrative team will give this report.
- Questions and Concerns from Members. Limit the amount and time.
- Summary of Main Points and Closing Prayer.

Foster a positive atmosphere during the member's meeting, and minimize conflict. Contentious and topics may be resolved in an officer's board meeting. For the member's meeting, focus on topics mentioned above.

16
CONDUCTING A BOARD MEETING

Local church board officers have the same standards as stipulated for deacons in 1 Timothy 3:8-13.

- Demonstrate godly living.
- Good report in and outside the church.
- Clear faithfulness to the church and its leadership.
- Maintain healthy family relationships.
- Faithfully give tithes and offering.
- Should not be a new believer; have been a faithful church member for at least three (3) years.
- Active participant in the church.

The senior pastor and the officer's board may appoint new members of the board. The members of the church may nominate one-fourth of the board. Follow the guidelines of your church's bylaws.

The officer's board advises and decides on matters of church business, plans, policy, and personnel. The officer's board may convene to discuss and make decisions on dealing with internal conflicts, legal matters and matters of church discipline.

Basic Agenda of a Board Meeting

1. Welcome, Prayer, Scripture Reading and Declaration of the Opening of the Meeting

    o The meeting should only begin if there is a quorum. A quorum is a majority of the Officers of the board. Official meetings should only proceed if a majority of the decision-making members are present to vote. A majority is equal to half of the number of officers plus one. For example, the majority of a board of 8 members would be 5. If a quorum is not reached, present officers may discuss matters; but legally, binding decisions cannot be made.

2. Apologies for Absences

    o The secretary shares reasons for any absences with apologies.

3. Reading of the Minutes of the Previous Meeting

    o The minutes are comprehensive recordings of the proceedings of a meeting. The minutes serve as legal records. Minutes include a list of all the meeting's attendees, the time of the meeting, discussions of the issues, responses to the discussion, and decisions that are made. Minutes of the previous meeting should be read at each meeting.

4. Correction of the Minutes

    - After reading the minutes, the secretary or chairman asks for corrections of the minutes, and then for the confirmation of the minutes.
    - Now, officers that were present at the previous meeting can present any corrections to be made to the minutes.
    - After raising a correction, the officers may deliberate on whether to accept or reject the modification.
    - A correction is accepted if there is no further motion to amend (all officers agree to the correction).

5. Confirmation of the Minutes

    - After all corrections are made, an officer moves to confirm the minutes. Then the chairman or secretary asks for a second motion to confirm the minutes. An officer will then move to second the confirmation of the minutes. (Minutes are only deemed official upon being confirmed). Note: if a correction needs to be made after confirmation of the minutes, an officer must call a motion to amend. Then the amendment would have to be seconded and again confirmed by the board.

6. Matters Arising from the Minutes
   - Chairman asks the board if anyone has any matter to put before the board that arises from the minutes.

7. Reports
   - Board officers or committees will report on matters from previous meetings and or on ongoing operations.

8. New Business
   - The chairman or the senior pastor/leader brings new business to the board.

9. Other Business
   - The senior pastor/leader or the chairman may open for any officer to raise other business. Other business is not related to the main business discussed in the meeting and would not need an extended length of time.

10. Adjourning of the Meeting
    - State the next steps and close in prayer.

For best practice, hold an officer's board meeting at least twice per year, or once per quarter.

17
TIPS FOR RESOLVING CONFLICTS

Barnabas supported the Apostle Paul when some in the early church were skeptical of his ministry. Yet, Barnabas and Paul separated because of a disagreement about taking John on the journey (Acts 15:35-41). Conflicts will occur. Many are due to human faults and others from different perspectives. While demonic spirits inspire some, others stem from sinful intentions. Pastors should foster a culture that deals with general conflicts Biblically.

- Teach leaders and members to follow the Biblical principle for offenses (Matthew 18:15-18).
  - If a brother offends you, bring the matter to your brother. Forgive the brother who repents.
- If the brother does not respond favorably to your correction, bring two or three witnesses from the church. The witnesses should be mature members of the church. With a positive response from the brother, the matter has been settled.
- If the brother does not hear even with the witnesses, then take the matter to the church.

From here, bring the matter to the pastoral leadership. Follow any instructions given by the pastoral leadership. At this point, leave the matter to be dealt with corporately under the leadership of the pastoral team.

- Establish explicit procedures for reporting disagreements and grievances. The general procedure is:
  - Bring any grievance or disagreement to an immediate leader. Generally, it may be a department leader or a minister in the church.
  - If a person is not satisfied with the action of an immediate leader, then he/she may take the matter to a more senior leader, which may be one of the pastors, or to the senior pastor.
  - Beyond the senior pastor, bring matters to a regional or organizational leader in the church body.
- Try to deal with conflicts privately. Avoid any public arguments at all costs.
- For grievances and accusations against ministers and leaders, seek for credible corroboration of the matter with at least two witnesses before taking any action. While taking the person's complaint seriously, no further action should be taken against the minister when accusations are uncorroborated (1 Timothy 5:19).

- Pastors and ministerial leaders should avoid making rash statements and decisions when a conflict is first brought up. Try to calm the person bringing the conflict to your attention. Let them know you will consider the matter. Seek wisdom from the Lord concerning the matter and investigate the problem further before resolving it

  (Proverbs 15:1, 18, 28; Proverbs 18:13).

- As led by the Lord, look over small conflicts. They often may resolve themselves, or the people involved may resolve the matter on their own. Like with Barnabas and Paul some conflicts are necessary for growth (Acts 15:35-41).

- Delegate some conflict resolutions to ministers and leaders who may have a better relationship with the persons involved in the conflict or may otherwise be better equipped to handle the problem.

- Consult the pastoral team or the officer's board for difficult conflicts. Furthermore, consult senior leaders in the church body (Proverbs 24:6).

- When a conflict arises and increases emotional tension (anger, frustration, anxiety, etc.), it is often best to step away from the situation until you are calm. Deal with the situation later. Avoid making rash statements stemming from anger.

HANDLING UNUSUAL OR DEMONIC CONFLICTS

Antagonists

At least one antagonist arises in every church. This is someone who opposes the leadership and direction of the church constantly. At first, they gain influence with the leaders and core workers of the church and may seem the most loyal. Then, the antagonist often begins with one complaint and "recruits" others in the church to see things their way. Despite the efforts of the leaders and workers to pacify the antagonists, they often find something else to complain about or someone else to accuse. If left unchecked, their efforts often lead to deep divisions in the church and or rebellion against the leader.

Jezebel Spirit

An antagonist is often a person who has experienced serious church or domestic hurt, is under demonic bondage, or has ongoing severe spiritual issues. They may begin as lite complainers and accusers but grow more rebellious when their spiritual needs are left unmet. If the pastoral team can recognize the spiritual issues in a rising antagonist, lead them to repentance, and minister to them, the problem may be abated. Otherwise, satan often takes advantage of the opening in the person's life and uses them. As a result, the Jezebel spirit will enter the heart of some.

The Jezebel spirit seeks to do the following: (1) gains influence with leaders – 2 Kings 21:8, 15 (2) undermines church leadership (3) makes divisive false accusations – 1 Kings 21:10 (4) brings in contrary teachings – Revelations 2:20 (5) condones worldly and rebellious behavior - Revelation 2:20 (6) silences visionary voices of the church – 1 Kings 18:4, 13. Essentially, the Jezebel spirit uses the antagonists to divide the church, overthrow the leadership, and destroy the visionary direction and impact of the church.

What to Do?

The best defense and offense against the antagonistic behavior and Jezebel spirit is the unity of the church. Pastors must cultivate a culture of unity with leaders and core workers following the Biblical procedure when conflicts and offenses arise (Matthew 18:15 – 18). Unifying in response to the antagonist and the Jezebel spirit is the winning strategy. The leading of the Spirit is needed for these conflicts. Some general steps that can be taken are:

- o Identify rising antagonists who bring minor complaints and accusations that stem from past hurts, demonic bondages, and similar spiritual issues.

Tips for Resolving Conflicts

- Minister to potential antagonists. See the chapter on "How to Minister Deliverance".
- Avoid placing rising antagonists in key or influential positions in the church. Even if they received deliverance, they would still need to prove themselves before placing them in any key roles.
- Be watchful of potential antagonists. The best way to do this is to develop a culture where complaining, contrary, and accusatory words and behavior are reported.
- Teach the core leaders and workers to identify rising troublemakers and to block them from causing division. The goal is to give them no room.
- Pastors should ensure that they build and train the officer's board of the church to act in unity when faced with opposition from antagonists. The officer's board comprises leaders who have years of proven loyalty and are definitively on board with the church's doctrine and direction.
- Identify antagonists with the officer's board first, and prayerfully discuss steps to deal with them. The response must be a unified one. Correct antagonists at this level first before exposing the matter to a larger group.
- Plan a response that everyone understands and agrees to. The response identifies the positives

of the church and its leadership in countering the antagonist's accusations. Also include the unbiblical actions and statements that the antagonists are making. Be ready to state what action you will ask the antagonist to make: repent, recant, renounce, or even remove themselves from the church.
- Once a person is being antagonistic and have rejected an initial attempt to correct them, bring the matter to the leadership team and or board of the church. Again, have a clear unified response.
- Firmly teach and preach against the actions and falsehoods being spoken by the antagonist. For example, preach on false accusation, false teachings, division, etc.
- Forcefully come against the Jezebel spirit at work against the church. Make it a united front. Call for corporate prayer by the leaders and the church against the spirit.
- Alert the officer's board to look out for victims, sympathizers, and accomplices to the antagonist.
- Lovingly minister to the victims showing them the wrongs of the antagonists using the Word of God.
- Sharply correct the sympathizers showing them from the Word of God how their actions or

words are creating division. Be ready to defend the ministry. Have a unified response.
- Do not be afraid to lose a few. The antagonist may leave. Some leaders who were accomplices may leave. Some victims may leave. Do not be afraid to correct antagonists and rebuke the Jezebel spirit because somebody may leave the church.

The Jezebel spirit banks on the leader being intimidated or reluctant to stand against her. Those with antagonistic behavior will often play on calling for the leaders and church to "show love". Unitedly, speak the truth in love. Do not back down from addressing antagonistic behavior in the name of love. Instead, bring your officer's board and leadership on board with a unified response against antagonism and the Jezebel spirit.

18
HANDLING CHURCH FINANCES

It is incumbent upon pastors to manage church finances with the utmost diligence. One key thing to remember is that church funds belong to the Lord; it is for the work of the Lord. Therefore, it is a mistake for pastors to deal with the church's finances as if it is his or her own. Indeed, this would mean not pocketing the church offering. However, it also means that the pastor is not the sole source of financial funding for the church. Thus, effective leadership in the church's financial management means that the pastor must incorporate the church's leaders and members in taking responsibility for the funding and administration of the church's money.

Senior pastors and the pastoral team should avoid directly handling money. The pastor must be above reproach in handling church funds. The pastor's role is to receive reports and monitor the financial health of the church. The pastor should ensure that the church funds are being used primarily to advance the church's vision, and that funds are being managed with fidelity.

Every church should appoint a financial or treasury team of at least two to three people to count, record, deposit money, and do transactions. The financial team submits a report to the pastor. If the financial team is not available, appoint other administrative workers or deacons to the role.

Necessary Protocols

Establish a protocol where at least two people always handle, count, deposit, and record offerings, tithes, and donations. The two people that are handling the funds should not be from the same family. Additionally, it is best, where possible, to avoid having more than one of the pastor's family members on the financial team.

The pastor should instruct the financial team to follow all legal protocols in recording and reporting income from giving. Pastors should see a report of income and expenses weekly. Generally, the financial team should complete monthly or quarterly reports of the church's income and expenses. And a yearly report should be kept. Traditionally, the consensus has been to keep financial reports for at least seven years; however, it is only necessary to follow the local legal recommendations. In the United States, the IRS recommends keeping records for four years (https://www.irs.gov/pub/irs-pdf/p1828.pdf). It is best to have an official accountant look over the financial records at least once a year to ensure it is in line with best practices and to produce an official report of the church's finances.

Increase Giving

Teach the church to give. Give a short motivational teaching or sermon when the offering is being collected to remind the congregation of the Biblical command to give. Also, give sufficient time for the congregation to give their offering. While not abusing the time spent on offering, also avoid rushing the offering. The church should understand that giving is a pivotal part of the worship service.

Testimonies and Reports

When possible, allow members to share their testimonies of God's financial blessings in their lives. God is faithful to those who give diligently. Givers will see God's blessings in their lives. When they share their testimony of God 's blessings, others will be motivated to give.

In the same manner, the church should share with its members how funds are being used. When members see and hear about the impact of their giving, it will motivate them to give more. At least annually, it is a good practice to have the financial team share an official report of the church's income and expenses; do this in an official member's meeting of the church.

Reimbursements and Expense Fund

Any funds that are given to members of the church to cover an expense on behalf of the church should be carefully recorded. For best practices, based on the recommendations of the United States Internal Revenue Service (IRS), funds given to cover expenses should be accountable; meaning, that it should be directly tied to describable expenses. Therefore, record these funds explicitly. Receipts should be provided and kept. Or, have recipients sign off on the amount and purpose of any funds they receive. Reimbursements carry the same expectations.

Generally, teach and share with the church how the church finances are used. Include teaching the church the advantages of providing for the care of the pastor (1 Timothy 5:17-18, Galatians 6:6, 1 Corinthians 9:14, 1 Corinthians 9:18-19). A healthy church will take up the financial concerns of the church and see to funding the church's vision, paying overhead costs, and caring for the pastor.

19
LAYING ON OF HANDS

Although neglected by some, the laying on of hands is an impactful pastoral practice. The practice of laying hands goes back to the patriarchs. We see that Jacob laid hands on Ephraim to confer the firstborn's blessing him (Genesis 48:14, 18). Moses laid hands upon Joshua to ordain him as his successor in Numbers 27:18-23. Jesus and the apostles continued the practice in the New Testament. It is a prominent practice in the early church. Actually, as with baptism, it is a foundational doctrine and practice of the New Testament church (Hebrews 6:1-2). Traditionally, the practice entails laying hands on the head of the recipient.

The pastor should regularly lay hands for the following purposes.

To Minister the Gift of the Holy Spirit

Jesus baptizes the believer in the Holy Spirit, but the laying on of hands serves as a point of contact, a conduit, as God releases the gift of the Spirit. There are numerous scriptures in the New Testament where the laying on of hands serves as a point of contact for the administration of the Spirit (Acts 8:17; Acts 9:17; Acts 19:6).

To Confirm Spiritual Gifts

The pastor can lay hands on others to confirm the spiritual gift that operates in believers (1 Timothy 4:14; 2 Timothy 1:6).

To Minister Healing

Laying on of hands to minister healing is often emphasized in scripture (Mark 16:18; Luke 4:40). Although not specifically mentioned the laying on of hand seems implied in James 5:14 *Is any sick among you? let him call for the elders of the church; and let them pray over him, anointing him with oil in the name of the Lord.* In the statement, and let the elders "pray over him"; the praying over him may suggest the laying on of hands. In either case, Jesus regularly laid hands to minister healing (Luke 4:40; Luke 13:13; Mark 8:23; Mark 6:5).

To Dedicate Babies

Jesus gives us this example as he laid hands and blessed the children that were brought to him. Pastors can lay hands during the dedication ceremony. Laying hands upon babies to confer blessings upon them is not an act of salvation. The child must make a conscious decision of follow Christ at a proper age of consent. The laying on of hands upon the baby is to minister general blessings, well-being and favor upon the child.

To Confer Blessings

Jesus conferred blessings upon the children that were brought to him through the laying on of hands. Jacob also laid hands upon Ephraim and Manasseh and spoke blessings over them (Genesis 48:14). Through the laying on of hands, the pastor can speak blessings over congregants.

To Confirm Appointment to a Position

Your church body may designate other ecclesiastical and presbyterial leaders such as bishops, overseers, etc., to ordain individuals to a ministerial position (Acts 6:5-6, Acts 13:1-3). However, the pastor may appoint non-ministerial positions in the church and confirm the appointment by laying hands.

Cautions with Laying Hands

When the laying on of hands involves appointing or confirming someone to a position, the Bible warns not to do this hastily. If you lay hands upon someone to appoint or confirm them to a position, you bear some responsibility for any sinful activity in their life. By publicly laying hands on the person, you are placing some level of approval upon them, and therefore bearing some responsibility if the person is spreading false doctrine or living an immoral life. Thus, the pastor or presbyterial leader must have confidence in the person's integrity before laying hands upon them.

Similarly, pastors should avoid having other ministerial leaders, who they cannot vouch for, lay hands upon them. Receiving the laying on of hand from other ministers conveys some type of connection or identification with them or their ministry. Therefore, if the pastor allows a minister who teaches false doctrine or lives immorally to lay hands upon them, the pastor is allowing identification and connection with that false or immoral ministry. So just as the Bible says in *1 Timothy 5:22 Lay hands suddenly on no man, neither be partaker of other men's sins*, we can also say, let no man suddenly lay hands on you connecting you with their sins.

Matters of Ecclesiastical Seniority

The common and best practice is for senior ecclesiastical leaders to lay hands on other ministers and members. It is unusual and unadvisable for ministers or other lay leaders to lay hands on ecclesiastical leaders that are senior to them. For example, a minister should not suddenly lay hands on an overseer, or a bishop. The only possible exception to this would be if the senior leader requests for the other minister to lay hands on them. Instead of directly laying hands, one can pray for a senior leader in a variety of methods such as holding hands in agreement, stretching out hands toward the person, or simply praying for them without physical interaction.

In the same vein, pastors should avoid having other pastors suddenly lay hands upon them. As mutual shepherds ministering to a congregation, it is wise for pastors to get the permission from pastors on whom they want to lay hands. Otherwise, pastors can utilize other methods of praying for other pastors without directly laying hands upon them.

Methods of Laying Hands

- Traditionally placing a hand on the head of the person (Genesis 48:14; Leviticus 1:4).
- Placing hands on the area in need of healing.
  - *Mark 8:25 After that he put his hands again upon his eyes, and made him look up: and he was restored, and saw every man clearly.*
  - Also Mark 7:32-35
  - Of course, laying hands on the area in need of healing requires discretion. Wisely refrain from laying hands on private areas of the body, areas that may cause harm, areas that maybe seen as culturally inappropriate, or areas that may be seen as sexually inappropriate.

- Speaking the healing then laying hands.
  - *Luke 13:12-13 And when Jesus saw her, called her to him, and said unto her, Woman, thou art loosed from thine infirmity. And he laid his hands on her: and immediately she was made straight, and glorified God.*
- Laying hands then speaking.
  - *Mark 10:16 And he took them up in his arms, put his hands upon them, and blessed them.*
- Praying first and then laying hands.
  - *Acts 8:15-17 Who, when they were come down, prayed for them, that they might receive the Holy Ghost: 16(For as yet he was fallen upon none of them: only they were baptized in the name of the Lord Jesus.) 17Then laid they their hands on them, and they received the Holy Ghost.*
- Laying hands twice.

*Mark 8:23-25 And he took the blind man by the hand, and led him out of the town; and when he had spit on his eyes, and **put his hands upon him**, he asked him if he saw ought. 24And he looked up, and said, I see men as trees, walking. 25After that he **put his hands again upon his***

***eyes**, and made him look up: and he was restored, and saw every man clearly.*

The laying on of hands is a foundational practice of the Christian faith. Pastors should neither neglect nor abuse it. Practice laying hands to impart healing, blessings, the baptism of the Spirit, and spiritual gifts, among the other things previously mentioned. However, it should not be abused: treating it as a mere ritual with no potency. Rather, pastors should build the people's faith to expect God to move when he lays hands on them. Then, the pastor should expect an impartation to take place when he lays hands. The touch of faith in God causes a transference. Interestingly many Jews sought for Jesus to lay hands on them or touch them; they believed in the doctrine of the laying on of hands (Mark 8:22, Mark 7:32, Mark 5:22-23; Matthew 19:13). Similarly, if we apply this practice with faith and expectation, it will produce mighty results.

20
MISCELLANEOUS SUGGESTIONS AND ADMONITIONS

GUEST SPEAKERS

Utilize guest speakers to supplement the church's giftset, especially during special events such as revivals, conferences, conventions, etc. Additionally, you can use guest speakers with the same giftset as the church to reinforce the ministry. However, avoid using guest speakers to replace regular pastoral preaching and teaching. The pastoral team should feed the flock.

Choose guest speakers whose giftset aligns with the purpose of an event. For example, it may best to have evangelistic preachers for revivals instead of teachers. Also, choose guest preachers who supplement the giftset of the pastoral team. For example, if the pastoral team does not have the gift of healing, it may be beneficial to invite speakers with this gift. Furthermore, you can choose guest speakers that have a similar giftset as the pastoral team to reinforce the ministry.

Always seek God's direction before inviting a guest speaker. Get recommendations from trusted leaders that you know. Avoid inviting anyone that you are uncomfortable about in doctrine or character; remember, whatsoever is not of faith is sin, so if you don't have assurance, do not invite the speaker.

It may be necessary to correct a doctrine or a statement made by a guest speaker. Often, in less severe infractions, this can be done at a later time with the congregation. For blatant heresy, there would be a need to correct the matter with the congregation immediately. Following, let the visiting minister know that the church does not agree with his doctrine without arguing or opening the door for debate.

Always be diligent to share your protocols and expectations with guest speakers before they minister. These protocols may include attire, sermon time, whether or not they should lay hands upon the people, raise offerings, etc.

PASTORAL SELF-CARE

The following are some practical tips for the pastor to take care of himself. Pastors should also teach their leadership team, workers, and members to assist. The church can ease much of the burden from the pastor, so that she can focus on spending time with God, preaching the word, and leading the church strategically to accomplish its vision.

Spiritual Care

- Remember that the most important thing is to spend time with Jesus in prayer and the word (Mark 3:14).
- Designate a place and a regular time when you pray and fellowship with God through His word (Matthew 14:23; Luke 5:16; 6:12).
- Do not confuse ministry performance with spiritual maturity.
- Evaluate your spiritual maturity by your obedience to God's Word and fellowship with Christ.
- Have scriptures at your fingertips that will encourage and build your spirit when things are low. Use them during those low times (Psalm 56:4).
- Record the revelations of your calling to ministry. Remind yourself of them when you are discouraged (Galatians 1:13-24).
- Ensure that there is someone in your life who you can go to with spiritual struggles that you may have, or if you fall into a sin (James 5:16).
- Surround yourself with people who can hold you accountable.
- Keep strict boundaries that will prevent you from committing egregious sins. Repent and self-correct

when you break the strict boundary, keeping you far from sinful activity (2 Corinthians 7:1; 2 Timothy 2:20-22).

Physical Care

- After ministering heavily, pull away from the crowd to pray and rest. Praying and resting refresh your physical body (Mark 6:31).
- Apply healthy eating habits (Mark 6:31).
- Study your body and your health. Maintain a diet that keeps you energetic and healthy.
- Rest after traveling extensively.
- Take advantage of leisure times to rest, such as being on a long flight, etc. (Matthew 8:24).
- Put limits on your time. Do not allow people to take over your schedule.

Managing Time with Family

- Designate specific times for your wife. Ensure that you please her emotionally and physically.
- Designate specific times to spend with your children.
- Avoid taking phone calls during designated time with family. Ministry calls can often get involved and take a lot of time.
- Involve your family in your ministry activities as much as possible.

- Travel with your wife on ministry tasks and endeavors as much as possible (1 Corinthians 9:5).
- Never make ministry or spiritual tasks an excuse for neglecting sexual intimacy with your spouse (1 Corinthians 7:5).
- Your first ministry is to your home. If you are not ministering to your home, and leading it effectively, you cannot pastor the church effectively (1 Timothy 3:5).
- Minister to your home. Pray for them. Lay your hands on them. Take time to hear about their issues and encourage them as necessary.

Managing a Secular Job and Ministry

- Do the secular job from the heart as unto the Lord. Be as joyful on the secular job as much as possible (Colossians 3:23).
- Distant yourself from the secular job when doing ministry activities or when you are home.
- Share your available times with the other pastors, ministers, and workers in the church.
- Delegate matters to others on the pastoral or leadership team of the church. Let them be your hands and feet when you are occupied with your secular job.
- Maximize all available holidays, vacation times, etc. to focus on the ministry, and spend time with family.

- Take personal days and sick days as necessary to manage your physical and mental health.
- Create a schedule for ministry work. If you have a full-time secular job, at a minimum, commit to a strong part-time schedule for the ministry or up to the hours of a second full-time job.
- Designate times to pray and study the Bible when there are no distractions from family, church, or work.

RELATING TO THE PEOPLE

Be Pastoral without Being Intrusive – visit the sick and grieving. Pray for people in time of need. Counsel those who need counseling. Otherwise, do not push into the personal lives of the people when not invited. Through the power of the Holy Spirit, allow the preaching and teaching of the Word of God to change the lives of the people.

Be Professional without Being Impersonal – maintain a pastoral office and allow congregants to set appointments. Send out an official letter, memos, emails, etc., as needed. Use a secretary to communicate on your behalf. Maintain a sense of high-quality professionalism. At the same time, show personality with the people: shake hands, know and refer to people by name, celebrate important moments and accomplishments in the lives of the people, take the time to talk with them, etc.

Set Boundaries. Set boundaries in your relationship with the people:

- Avoid being alone with the opposite sex. Take necessary precautions to avoid sexual temptation or accusation. Where possible, have a second minister with you for counseling sessions. If this is not possible, have someone close to the premises. Keep the office door open when speaking to someone of the opposite sex. Entirely avoid going to the home of someone of the opposite sex alone.

- Delegate some pastoral duties such as home visitations, hospital visits, etc. Many pastors burn out by trying to meet all the needs of the people themselves. Raise up other ministers and church leaders to assist with and take up these pastoral duties.

- Watch your time. Be caring and compassionate without allowing parishioners to overrun your time with their needs. Minister to them according to the leading of the Lord and then move on to others. Many have needs.

- Do not participate in the sins of others through collusion, consent, or silence (knowing but silently allowing).

Build Key Relationships – As led by the Lord, building a closer spiritual relationship with key people in the church is beneficial. Some of these may include:

- Pastoral team and ministerial leaders
- Departmental Leaders
- Influential laypeople in the church
- Prayer warriors.
- With the voices of the vision. Those in the church who consistently speak on and advocate for the vision of the church.

Develop and Mentor Others in the Ministry

Look out for laypeople who may be called to the ministry that you may train and mentor for greater service.

Know Your Church

- Get to know the gifts and abilities of the members in the church. You must know what is unique about the set of people in your church.
- Get to know the prominent supporters and gap-fillers in the church.
- Get to know the new believers and members. Many churches bypass them.
- Know who the main gossipers, the naysayers, and the criticizers are.

- Know the internal enemies. Jesus was aware of Judas.
- Get to know the general giving taking place in the church. A general increase in giving may signal spiritual growth and development in the church. Similarly, a decrease in giving may signal a spiritual decline in the church or ministry.

GENERAL RECOMMENDATIONS ON PANDEMICS AND DISASTERS

These recommendations are general. For more specific recommendations for the recent COVID-19 pandemic, contact us at hais@harvestarmy.org. Upon this book's publishing, the COVID-19 pandemic has significantly waned. However, these general recommendations are for upcoming pestilences that my come upon the earth.

- Be sensitive to the voice of God for revelations about upcoming disasters (Amos 3:7). You can connect with prophetic ministries that may also release warnings. Make preparations whenever God reveals a coming pestilence (Acts 11:28-29).
- Make the best effort to obey the Word of God to gather together (Hebrews 10:25, Psalm 133:1, Matthew 18:20, Acts 2:42, Hebrews 3:13) while taking all the necessary common sense and government-issued precautions.

Miscellaneous Suggestions and Admonitions

- Avoid the two extremes. One extreme is to ignore all medical precautions and government mandates. The other extreme is closing down the church and refusing to gather.
- When local conditions and or laws prevent regular services, endeavor to gather in some format. For example, gather in small groups over various different times and encourage others to view online. Tell the most vulnerable to stay home while the rest gather. Hold services in the church's parking lot or another outdoor venue.
- Develop an underground solution for gathering and holding services among the faithful. These may be unknown locations or times.
- Create a general plan of response to pandemics and disasters include communication strategies and systems, multiple methods of holding services, and methods of raising offerings. Determine which activities should be halted, and prioritize gathering for worship, fellowship, and preaching.
- In a disaster or pandemic, provide spiritual services to the community; for example, a prayer line, virtual meetings, temporary day shelter, food pantry, etc.
- Be aggressive in staying in contact with all members of the church during pandemics and

disasters. Have a system in place where leaders can easily call, support, and connect members.
- Use online and digital mediums as a supplement to minister to members, but not as a replacement for gathering.
- Abundantly prepare for pandemics and disasters with necessary kits and supplies. Build a food pantry with emergency meals and non-perishable goods.
- Remain open to the voice of God. Stay in touch with prophetic ministries.

Many other areas can be covered, but what is written is sufficient as a tool in pastoral ministry and leadership. If you have questions or want a topic to be added to an upcoming version of the manual, please email hais@harvestarmy.org.

BIBLIOGRAPHY

The following works were consulted in putting this manual together.

Collins, K. D. (2002). *The witnessing revolution.* Maitland, Florida: Xulon Press.

Kennedy, D. J., & Stebbins, T. (1996). *Evangelism explosion: equipping churches for friendship, evangelism, discipleship, and healthy growth.* Wheaton, IL: Tyndale House Publishers.

Murphy, E. F. (2003). *The handbook for spiritual warfare.* Nashville: T. Nelson.

Reid, Omaudi (2019). *The prophetic revolution.* New York: Harvesters Online Publishing.

Segler, F. M. (1969). *The Broadman ministers manual.* Nashville: Broadman Press.

Warren, Rick (2008). *The Purpose-driven Church What on Earth Is Your Church Here For?* Grand Rapids, Michigan: Zondervan.

www.ingramcontent.com/pod-product-compliance
Lightning Source LLC
Chambersburg PA
CBHW060318050426
42449CB00011B/2544